About the author

Patrick McMahon has been working in the field of English language teaching since 1987. He has worked as a teacher, a teacher trainer, a lecturer and materials writer in the UK and around the world. He currently lectures and is Academic Manager in the English Language Centre at Plymouth University. His recent work is in the area of English for Academic Purposes: teaching, lecturing and carrying out research into international students at British universities. *Collins Academic Skills Series: Group Work* is his first book.

Acknowledgements

I would like to thank my editor Rod Webb for doing more than an editor should be asked to do. I am grateful to Nick Robinson for making it happen. I need to thank Helen Bowstead, Qavitha Buspanathan and Qian Chen who gave me the benefit of their experiences in interviews. Thanks too to all at HarperCollins. I also want to thank my family – Clare, Alice, Harry and Fred – for their patience and encouragement.

Contents

Contents

POWERED BY COBUILD

Introduction

Collins Academic Skills Series: Group Work will give you the skills you need to take part in successful group work activities at university and college.

Designed to be used on a self-study basis to support English for Academic Purposes or study skills courses, it is intended for students on pre-sessional or Foundation courses as well as for first year undergraduate students.

The book has twelve chapters which cover the most important aspects of working with other students. You will learn:

- why group work is important
- how to prepare for group work and group assignments
- how to work collaboratively
- how different students learn and how to apply this knowledge to group work
- how to deal with difficult students
- how to write and present in groups
- how to reflect and learn from your group work experience.

At the back of the book there is:

- a list of useful phrases for group work
- transcripts of interviews with students on their experiences of group work
- transcripts of interviews with lecturers on their thoughts about group work
- a list of the skills, abilities and qualities needed for group work
- an example of a group presentation
- a glossary of key terms
- a comprehensive answer key

Chapter structure

Each chapter includes:

- Aims – These set out the skills covered in the chapter.
- A self-evaluation quiz – By doing this you are able identify what you already know on the subject of the chapter and what you need to learn.
- Information on academic expectations – These sections will help you understand university practices and expectations so you understand what is required.
- Practical exercises – These help you to develop the skills to succeed at university. You can check your answers at the back of the book.
- Tips – Key points are highlighted for easy reference and provide useful revision summaries for the busy student.

- Glossary – Difficult words are glossed in boxes next to the section where they appear in the chapter. There is also a comprehensive glossary at the back of the book.
- Remember sections – This is a summary of key points for revision and easy reference.

Glossary boxes ⊑ POWERED BY COBUILD

Where we feel that a word or phrase is difficult to understand, we have glossed this word/phrase. All definitions provided in the glossary boxes have been taken from the *COBUILD Advanced Dictionary*. At the end of the book there is a full alphabetical list of the most difficult words from the book for your reference.

Using *Group Work*

You can either work through the chapters from Chapter 1 to Chapter 12 or you can choose the chapters and topics that are most useful to you. The Contents page will help in your selection.

Study tips

- Each chapter will take between two to three hours. Take regular breaks and do not try to study for too long. Thirty to sixty minutes is a sensible study period.
- Regular study is better than occasional intensive study.
- Read the chapter through first to get an overview before you do any exercises. This will help you to see what you want to focus on.
- Try the exercises before referring to the Answer key. Be an active learner.
- After doing the exercises in the book, put what you have learned into practice when you are given real group work to do. The exercises will prepare you for group work but they are also examples of exercises you should do to make your group work successful.
- All university departments are different. Use the information in the book as a guide to understanding your own university department.
- Write questions you can ask to find out how your department expects you to work in groups.
- There is no one correct way of working with others. Use the experience you gain from doing the exercises to learn what works best for you. Adapt the suggestions in this book to suit your learning style and context.
- Learning to work in groups is an on-going process, which means you need to practise the same skills many times. Revise regularly.

Other titles

Also available in the *Collins Academic Skills Series: Lectures, Numbers, Presenting, Research* and *Writing*.

1 | Why do group work?

? Quiz
Self-evaluation

Read the statements and circle the answers that are true for you.

1	I prefer to work on my own rather than as part of a team.	agree | disagree | not sure
2	I can work as part of a team when I need to.	agree | disagree | not sure
3	When I work with other students, I make sure they follow what I say.	agree | disagree | not sure
4	I can learn everything I need to know from books and teachers; other students are not important.	agree | disagree | not sure
5	Other students may have different ideas; these ideas can challenge mine and make me think more.	agree | disagree | not sure
6	The final piece of work is the most important thing; the process of how the work is done is not.	agree | disagree | not sure

Now check the key for comments on this exercise.

What is group work?

Glossary

assignment
An assignment is a task or piece of work that you are given to do, especially as part of your job or studies.

Group work involves working with other students who are on the same course as you to complete a task or an assignment. You will find that lecturers in English-speaking universities often ask you to carry out work in groups.

There are different types of tasks and assignments that you can do when you work together. Some of them may be quite short, for example:

- holding group discussions

- checking your answers in groups.

Group discussions are usually held between small numbers of students and it is common practice for the lecturer to ask one group member to report their discussion to the whole class. Other group work activities may take more preparation, for example:

- giving a group presentation

- writing a group assignment.

These tasks will probably involve meeting your group outside class to spend time working together. Some group work assignments may even last several weeks or months. Examples of these from Business Studies are:

- setting up and running a university-based business

- designing a product and the marketing campaign for it.

When you work in groups, you sometimes have the option of choosing your own group members; this means you might decide to work with friends. Alternatively, you may be told who to work with by the lecturer. Another option is to have a random selection process. The size of groups might be small with two, three or four students, or there could be ten or more.

For more information on forming a group, see Chapter 2.

Glossary

common practice
Common practice is a generally accepted way of doing something.

option
An option is something that you can choose to do in preference to one or more alternatives.

random
A random sample or method is one in which all the people or things involved have an equal chance of being chosen.

Tips

Tips

✓ Try not to feel nervous when working in a group with people you do not know; use it as an opportunity to meet new people and make friends.

✓ Use the opportunity of working with others to develop your English language speaking skills, as well as to get help when you are not sure what to do.

Reasons why university students work in groups

Understanding the *purpose* of working in groups will motivate you to participate. This is important as a high percentage of your marks at university will come from group work. If you do not understand the reasons for working with others, it is unlikely you will participate well. University lecturers generally believe that:

- you can learn more about a topic when working in a group than when working alone

- teamwork skills are very important and can only be learned through group participation

- the most important part of learning happens while you are working with other students, not when working alone

- group work is an important preparation for the world of work as you will need to collaborate with colleagues in your professional life after university.

Exercise 1

Compare what happens in group work assignments in an English-speaking university with what happens in your own country. Read the statements and tick the columns that are true for you.

University assignments	English-speaking universities		My country	
	True	False	True	False
1 Group work is a popular way of setting work for students.				
2 Lecturers expect students to spend time working together outside class.				
3 Lecturers encourage students to discuss ideas in groups and to learn from each other.				
4 Students listen to each other and appreciate each other's points of view.				
5 Students take responsibility for finding out what they need to learn and learning it on their own.				

Now check the key for answers and comments on this exercise.

What is the value of working with other students?

As already stated, lecturers in English-speaking universities believe you will learn more when you work with other students than when you work alone. The following example of a group work assignment will help you to think about whether you agree or not.

For example: *Identify a shopping mall in the city and carry out a survey of its customers' shopping habits.*

There will be a number of stages to this assignment. The first stage might be to do some background reading on people's shopping habits. The information below shows how much you could do if you worked individually compared with working as part of a group.

Stage 1: Find out as much as you can about people's shopping habits by doing some background reading.

As individual work
- You can read a small number of articles and gain *some* information.

- Result: You have a small amount of information.

As group work
- Each group member can read different articles. Students can then meet and share their information with each other.

- Result: You have a lot of information.

The next stage might be to design a survey and write questions to ask shoppers. As before, this task will be easier to do as part of a group rather than done individually.

Stage 2: Write a list of questions to ask shoppers about their shopping habits.

As individual work
- You write all the questions you can think of.

- Result: You have a list of all the questions you could think of.

As group work
- Each group member writes a list of questions. You then work together to choose the *best ones*; some students have written good questions you did not think of.

- Result: You have a list of the best questions from each student.

The final stage might be to carry out the survey by stopping shoppers in the shopping mall. You can see from the information on page 12 how many shoppers you can ask on your own compared to working in a group.

Glossary

available
If something you want or need is available, you can find it or obtain it.

representative
A group of people or things is representative of a larger group of people or things if it closely matches the wider group.

refine
If something such as a process, theory or machine is refined, it is improved by having small changes made to it.

Stage 3: Carry out a survey of shoppers in a shopping mall.

As individual work	As group work
■ You ask as many shoppers as you can in the time you have.	■ You and your group members split up and go to different parts of the shopping mall. You ask as many shoppers as you can in the time available and then share all your information.
■ Result: You have a small number of respondents.	■ Result: You have a large number of respondents and your survey will be more representative.

You will have seen from these examples that there are clear advantages to working in groups.

- You learn more when you can share information that you get separately; it takes *time* to find and read information, but it does not take long to share this information with someone else.

- You learn from the ideas of others; you will have some ideas, but you cannot think of everything on your own. Other students will usually have some ideas you did not think of.

- You will benefit from explaining your ideas and listening to the ideas of other students. They will help you to see things from different points of view and help you to refine your ideas.

Exercise 2

Read the tasks below and make notes about the benefits of group work.

Task	Benefits of doing task in a group
Make a poster explaining the content of your degree programme for a university open day.	
Give a presentation entitled *The advantages of studying abroad for your degree*.	
Design a new product to sell at your university shop and persuade the shop manager to stock it.	

Now check the key for comments on this exercise.

What are teamwork skills and how do they help the process of learning?

As we have discussed, group work will help you to develop your teamwork skills, and teamwork skills are important for working effectively with other students. If you have good teamwork skills, you will be able to work collaboratively; your group will *achieve more* and *your marks will be higher*. Furthermore, specific marks for teamwork are often given for group assignments.

Look at the teamwork skills involved in the following group assignment.

> **For example:** *Set up and run a project for the design and implementation of an infrastructure project of your choice.*

Task stages	Teamwork skills you will practise
Deciding what infrastructure project your group will work on	<ul><li>Brainstorming</li><li>Listening to others</li><li>Making suggestions</li><li>Putting forward a point of view</li><li>Negotiating</li><li>Making group decisions</li></ul>
Making a list of student roles and responsibilities needed to complete the assignment and sharing them out	<ul><li>Problem-solving</li><li>Negotiating</li><li>Putting forward an opinion and supporting it</li><li>Allocating responsibilities</li><li>Recognizing the strengths of others</li></ul>
Drawing up a plan of the project	<ul><li>Problem-solving</li><li>Helping each other</li><li>Making suggestions</li><li>Sharing ideas</li><li>Collaborating</li></ul>

These are just some of the teamwork skills you might use, but there are many more (see Appendix 4 for a complete list). You will need to practise and use these skills when you work with others.

For more information on working collaboratively, see Chapter 4.

Tips

✓ Recognize that whenever your lecturer asks you to do something, there is a good reason for it.

✓ Reflect on what you are learning every time you do a task or assignment in order to get better marks.

Exercise 3

Read the assignments below. Which ones would be good for individual work, and which ones would benefit from teamwork? Write I if you think they are good for individual work and G if they would benefit from group work. What teamwork skills are needed to complete the group work assignments effectively?

Task	I / G	If group work, what teamwork skills are needed?
1 Make a video about student life in your university for the student union to show future students.		
2 Write a personal statement to apply for a placement in a company to gain work experience.		
3 Write a newspaper article explaining why students from abroad come to study at your university.		
4 Plan a *Welcome Event* for new students who are joining your course next term.		
5 Write a 500-word essay saying why you chose your degree programme and what you hope to gain from your studies.		

Now check the key for answers and comments on this exercise.

How is group work assessed as a process as well as a product?

Glossary

reflective
If you are reflective, you are thinking deeply about something.

enable
If someone or something enables you to do a particular thing, they give you the opportunity to do it.

University lecturers also ask you to work with others because of the skills and subject knowledge you gain during the group work process. This means that the lecturers are not only interested in the finished assignment that you hand in, they are also interested in *what happened* when you were working on the assignment; they will give you marks for this process of working as well as marking your final assignment. This is why the *process* is important, not just the product. If the product is good but only one person worked on the assignment, you will score poorly on the collaborative working part of the assignment.

In long assignments there are usually several parts, for example, a group presentation as well as individual writing. It is common to include a reflective piece of writing in which you show what you have learned from your group work. This enables you to make comments about how you worked as a group and how you solved any problems that came up.

For more information on reflective writing, see Chapter 9.

Remember

✓ You can usually achieve more when working in a group than working individually.

✓ University lecturers will expect you to participate actively in group work.

✓ University lecturers want to see you listening to and learning from other students.

✓ You get marks for being a good group member.

✓ If your final assignment looks good but your group work is poor, you might be disappointed with your mark.

2 Preparing for group work

Aims ✓ learn ways of forming a group and getting to know each other

✓ recognize the value of team-building activities

✓ assign roles and responsibilities, establish rules and share contact information

✓ create a shared digital workspace

? Quiz
Self-evaluation

Read the statements and circle the answers that are true for you.

1	I want to be able to choose my own group members.	agree | disagree | not sure
2	I think it is much easier to work with people who have the same nationality as me.	agree | disagree | not sure
3	Team-building activities can be useful to build a strong group.	agree | disagree | not sure
4	I don't like having a lot of rules; I prefer a more relaxed approach to work.	agree | disagree | not sure
5	I think everyone should help each other, so individual responsibilities are not important.	agree | disagree | not sure

Now check the key for comments on this exercise.

Forming a group

Glossary

constraint
A constraint is something that limits or controls what you can do.

There are a variety of ways of selecting the members of a group. For example, the lecturer can:

- decide on the members of each group; you do not have a choice

- allow you to choose your group members with complete freedom

- allow students to choose their group members, but give some constraints, for example numbers of males and females or the mix of nationalities

- use a random selection process, for example picking out names written on individual pieces of paper.

Your lecturer will generally have good reasons for choosing one of these methods. If you understand what these reasons are, you are likely to have a more successful group.

Exercise 1

Read the methods of selecting group members below. Make notes about the advantages and disadvantages of each one.

Method	Advantages	Disadvantages
1 The lecturer decides on the group members with no input from students.	*It is a quick way to choose the group. There are no arguments about the group members.*	
2 Students freely choose their own group members.		
3 Students can choose their group members within constraints given by the lecturer.		
4 Group selection is done through a random process.		*You might have all the students with similar skills in the same group.*

Now check the key for answers and comments on this exercise.

Tips   ✓   If you are unhappy about your group membership, try to make it work before asking to move.

           ✓   You should talk to your tutor or lecturer if you still feel uncomfortable in your group after a period of time.

Getting to know each other

It is very important for you and the other group members to get to know each other so you can work together effectively. If you have some basic information about them, you will quickly find shared interests and start to understand how they think and work.

The activities in Exercises 2, 3 and 4 are just some of the ones you might choose in order to learn something about the other members in your group. Your lecturer is unlikely to use such activities, but will assume that the group takes responsibility for organizing and carrying out this process.

Exercise 2

Look at the form below that a student has completed after meeting a new group member. The information is very basic. What follow-up questions can they ask to get more interesting information?

Nice to meet you!

Work in pairs. Take it in turns to ask each other the following questions. Make notes of the answers.

1 **Full name:** Narantuya Bayarmaa

2 **Name to be used in the group/Nickname:** Natalie

3 **Nationality:** Chinese

4 **First language:** Mongolian

5 **Languages you can speak:** Mongolian, Mandarin, English

6 **Currently living:** Shanghai

7 **Course:** Mechanical Engineering

8 **Reasons for choosing this course:** China needs engineers

9 **Hobbies:** Horse riding, swimming, travelling and learning about new cultures

10 **Plans following this course:** Return to China and work in the field of developing renewable energy

When you have finished come together as a group and introduce your partner to the rest of the group. Partners should give more information, correct the information being given, and ask and answer more questions. This will generate a rewarding 'getting to know each other' session.

Now check the key for answers and comments on this exercise.

Glossary

skills audit
A skills audit is a thorough check or examination of a person's skills and abilities.

A skills audit (see Exercise 3) is a useful way of finding out about the strengths and weaknesses of the various group members. It is very useful to exchange this information with your group so that you can decide who is best suited to each task.

Exercise 3

Read the skills audit form below and rate your skills. Write 1 if you think your skills need improvement, 2 if they are adequate and 3 if they are good.

Skills audit	
Skills	**Rate your skills 1 / 2 / 3**
1 *Written communication skills in English*: able to write fluently in English without making serious grammar mistakes	
2 *Spoken communication skills in English*: able to discuss things in English, give points of view and justify opinions	
3 *Pronunciation skills*: having good enough pronunciation so that people can easily understand you when you speak	
4 *Presentation skills*: able to give an adequate formal presentation in English in front of others	
5 *IT skills*: able to carry out a range of practical tasks using a variety of computer programmes such as word processing, digital presentations and making posters	
6 *Numeracy skills*: good with numbers when carrying out tasks such as costing, budgeting and keeping accounts	
7 *Teamwork skills*: able to work together with other students, negotiate compromise and share ideas	
8 *Reading and note-taking skills*: able to read long texts quickly and easily, understand them and take useful notes that can be understood later	

Now check the key for comments on this exercise.

Ice-breakers (see Exercise 4) are a useful type of activity to use when a group meets for the first time as they will help to make all the group members feel at ease with each other. In other words, they help to break the ice.

Exercise 4

Look at the ice-breaker activity on page 20 and answer the questions.

1   How easy would it be to complete?
2   How interesting would it be to use?
3   How useful would it be in terms of getting to know others?

Sharing experiences

1 Think about something you learned to do recently, e.g. driving or speaking another language.
    a Was it a good learning experience, or not?
    b What made it a good or a bad learning experience?

2 Think about a really good teacher that you had when you were at school.
    a What made this teacher special?
    b How did this affect the way you worked?

3 Think about a subject that you did not like at school.
    a What made you dislike the subject?
    b Could anything have been done to make it better?

4 Have you ever worked in a group before? If so:
    a What made it a good experience?
    b What did you learn from it?

5 Think about something you have done that needed courage and took you out of your comfort zone, for example, doing something for the first time, or doing something you did not like or did not want to do.
    a How did you face your fear of doing it?
    b What did you learn from it?

Now check the key for comments on this exercise.

Glossary

distribute
If you distribute things, you hand them or deliver them to a number of people.

It is important to make use of the various information you gather about the members of your group during any ice-breaking activities. It would therefore be useful to complete a table similar to the one below.

For example:

Group skills overview		
Group member's name	Has particular skills in ...	Has experience of ...

After sharing the information, you can ask one group member to type it up and distribute it to the rest of the group. The group can then use the information to help allocate roles and tasks that need to be covered in your group work.

Team-building activities

Even when students already know each other, it is important to improve communication skills and build trust within a group. In professional life, many companies organize team-building activities for their staff. These activities can be simple ones, for example:

- having a meeting or a conference
- having a meal
- going on a day trip.

The importance of team-building in profession life can be seen by the large amount of money some companies spend on team-building activities. These are often not connected with work in any way and include such things as:

- adventure sports (e.g. climbing, walking, boating)
- raft building
- cooking classes.

This emphasis on team building in professional life demonstrates why you should place importance on team building in your student life.

Exercise 5

Look at the team-building activities below. Which activities could be good for team building when the group members already know each other? Which ones would work best? Which of them might *not* be a good idea? Make notes.

Team-building activity	Would be good because ...	Might not be good because ...
1 Inviting the group for a meal where every member brings a dish from their country		
2 A visit to the local zoo		
3 A day out at a local theme park		
4 Planning and taking a day's walk in the countryside using maps and a picnic		

Now check the key for answers and comments on this exercise.

Understanding roles and responsibilities

As group work is designed to get the *best* out of the individuals that make up the group, it is essential that the group operates effectively. A group is more likely to be effective if each student has a particular role as well as the responsibilities that come with that role. It is also vital that each group member fully understands their role and their responsibilities.

Sometimes your lecturer will give you a list of formal roles that must be filled by the members of your group.

For example:

Role (or post)	Responsibilities	Skills and abilities used in this role
Group secretary	■ To take notes during group meetings ■ To write up the notes afterwards ■ To distribute them to the group ■ To prepare an agenda for group meetings ■ To distribute the agenda beforehand	This person would need good note-taking skills; good communication skills; the ability to listen carefully; good organizational skills; efficiency; the ability to write up documents and distribute them quickly.

Exercise 6

Read the group work assignment below. How would you allocate the group roles and responsibilities in the table below? Make notes about the skills and abilities you think are used in the roles.

For example: *Design and produce a product for the baby market. Create an accompanying marketing campaign using a variety of different media.*

Role (or post)	Responsibilities
Group chair	To review overall progress on the assignment; to chair meetings; to settle disputes
Designer and developer	To design and produce the product so it is ready to be sold
Marketing and publicity officer	To design and execute a marketing campaign for the product
Accountant	To keep accounts for the group and to publish them
IT officer	To be in control of the IT needs of the group

Now check the key for answers and comments on this exercise.

Matching roles and responsibilities to the appropriate group member is
an important skill that requires an objective judgement of both your own
skills and those of the other group members.

Exercise 7

Read about the students below and think about the roles and responsibilities in
Exercise 6. Which person might be suitable for each role and why?

Fatimah	Often helps her friends with computer problems; runs a website for family business and uses many different computer programmes for a range of activities and hobbies including photography.
David	Interested in all sorts of technology and gadgets; good with his hands; a keen cyclist and regularly works on his bike to improve its performance.
Lora	Very efficient and well organized; popular with others; loves going out with friends and organizing parties and outings for them; good at helping others to sort out problems, so people often ask for her help; not very interested in creative tasks.
Jinjie	Academically very strong; has always done well in maths and science; has worked in parents' business and is comfortable using spreadsheet software and formulas for calculating rows of figures and creating charts and diagrams.
Eduardo	Very creative and artistic; loves drawing and painting; very good with technology and can use a wide range of computer software for many different uses.

Now check the key for answers and comments on this exercise.

Tips   ✓   When you start your group work, make a list of the roles and responsibilities for your
group.
✓   Think carefully about the role and responsibilities you would like to take on and be
prepared to tell the other students why you should take that role.
✓   If you find out after a while that you are not comfortable in your role, speak to your
group about it. But do not expect other students to swap roles with you after they have
started to work on things they are responsible for.
✓   Do not be embarrassed to ask other group members for help and support even though
you have responsibilities for a task. If you need support, others probably need it too.

Assigning roles and responsibilities

To help you to choose which members of your group should take on particular roles, you could make a role card for each one.

For example:

> **Role card**
>
> **Group secretary**
>
> **Main responsibilities:** Take notes during group meetings, write them up and distribute them to the group. Prepare an agenda for group meetings and distribute beforehand.
>
> **Skills needed:** Note-taking skills; a good eye for detail; well organized; good communication skills.

During the activity, you would place the role cards on the table in front of the group and discuss who would be good in each role. This would involve negotiation and the use of specific language. Use the following useful phrases to do this.

> **Negotiating**
>
> I'd really like to take on the role of ...
>
> I'd be good in the role of ... because I'm good at ...
>
> My experience in ... means that I'd make a very good ...
>
> I think David should be ... because he's ...
>
> I know you want that role but would you consider me for it?
>
> I don't think I'd be suitable for that. I'm not very good at ...
>
> I'm sorry. I'm really not keen on being ... How about if I take on ...?

Tip ✓ Keep any role cards you produce and bring them out at group meetings to help discuss who should be doing what.

Establishing rules

Glossary

ground rule
The ground rules for something are the basic principles on which future action will be based.

It is important to have some ground rules for your group work. Ground rules can prevent misunderstandings and keep your group on track.

For example:

> Group members must attend all meetings. If a member cannot attend a meeting, they must tell the group secretary at least 24 hours before the scheduled meeting time.

Exercise 8

Read about some common problems that can arise during group work. Suggest a ground rule for each problem. Make notes.

Problem	Ground rule to solve the problem
1 Some students are late or do not attend group meetings.	
2 Some students spend time talking on their phone or texting during meetings.	
3 Some students do not say anything in meetings.	
4 Some students are not sure what they are supposed to do after meetings.	
5 Some students interrupt other students when they are talking and want to talk all the time.	
6 Some students do not produce work on time.	
7 Some students talk to non-group members about confidential group matters.	
8 Some students are inflexible and want everybody to do things their way.	
9 Sometimes there is a long time between group meetings, so the group loses focus.	

Now check the key for answers and comments on this exercise.

For more information on how to deal with difficulties within your group, see Chapter 7.

Tips ✓ Remember to keep your list of ground rules close to hand so you can refer to it if you have some problems in your group.

✓ Think about what you will do if a group member breaks a ground rule and include this in the ground rules too!

Sharing contact information

You will need to share contact information with your group members and say how you would like to keep in touch with each other. Different students may prefer different methods and only be comfortable giving out certain information. It is therefore a good idea to include some rules about keeping in touch in your group's ground rules. Make sure that the information you give out is up to date and that you check regularly to see if your group members are trying to contact you.

Use a group contact form to collect and share your group's information.

For example:

Group contact form					
Name	Email address	Mobile number	Landline number	When not to call	Best way to get in touch

Tips ✓ You can use a form like the one above to share contact details among your group.
✓ Do not leave long periods of time without getting in touch with your group members as this is likely to result in problems.

Creating a shared digital workspace

You will need to create computer files in your group work and you should consider how you will store your work and share it with your group. There are a lot of different ways you can do this using online and offline technology. It is important to remember that:

- different students will have different IT skills

- different students will feel comfortable using different software.

The table on page 27 contains examples of different places where you can store your group work. It also includes a commentary on the advantages and disadvantages of different methods of storage.

For example:

Technology	What you can do with it	Advantages	Disadvantages
Memory stick	You can store your digital files on it.	It is easy to carry around.	You can lose a memory stick!
Folders on a shared computer drive at university or college	You can store, upload and download files to it.	Everyone can easily access all the files.	There may be restrictions accessing the shared drive when you are outside the institution.
Folders on a shared online drive	You can store, upload and download files to it. Some products can synchronise files across different computers.	You always have the latest version of the file and you do not need to use a memory stick or email.	For all these online options you need a fast and reliable internet connection and access to a reasonable computer.
Wiki	You can add content to a webpage and so share your work.	You can easily see each other's ideas, work on it and edit it together from different locations.	
An online message board	You can read and leave messages for each other.	It is an easy way for the group to share ideas when they are at different locations.	

Remember

✓ Group work gets easier as time goes on.

✓ It is worthwhile spending time to get to know your group members.

✓ Get to know the strengths of your group members so you can use each other's skills.

✓ Be prepared to negotiate for the role that you want in your group.

✓ Ground rules will help to keep your group on track.

3 Planning your group assignment

Aims
- ✓ understand how to interpret your assignment: what you are being asked to do
- ✓ understand the requirements of the task
- ✓ use a brainstorming technique to generate ideas
- ✓ learn techniques for scheduling your work
- ✓ recognize the importance of setting clear goals

Quiz
Self-evaluation

Read the statements and circle the answers that are true for you.

1	I don't have a clear idea of what the work will look like when it's finished; I just start and see where it goes.	agree | disagree | not sure
2	I don't usually read course documents that the lecturer gives out as I find them dull.	agree | disagree | not sure
3	I find it useful to work in a group and share ideas.	agree | disagree | not sure
4	I don't think you can plan too much in advance because you don't know how long the work will take.	agree | disagree | not sure
5	It's important to be flexible when you work.	agree | disagree | not sure

Now check the key for comments on this exercise.

Understanding the requirements of the task

It is essential to understand what your lecturer wants you to do in any group work assignment. One way of doing this is by asking questions about the assignment. Look at this task for Tourism students.

> **For example:** *Create a two-week adventure package holiday aimed at the young family market (two professional adults, two young children). Produce a marketing brochure to appear in travel agent outlets that includes details of destination, duration, accommodation, activities and costs. You will be asked to present your package holiday to the class and answer questions about it.*

28

You can use 'wh-questions' to help you to analyse the question and understand exactly what is required. It is a good idea to try and come up with questions using all seven question words.

What? When? Who? Why? Where? Which? How?

You can also use the following questions stems.

Can we …? Should we …? Do we have to …?

The same questions would help you to understand the task when working alone. However, when working in a group, you have the opportunity to *discuss them with others in the group* and, between you, arrive at a thorough understanding of the task.

Exercise 1

Read the example task on page 28. How many questions can you write to help you to understand the task? Think about the different elements of the task. Some questions have been given to help you.

1	Questions about your group	*Who will I work with?* *Can I …*
2	Questions about the brochure	*When does the brochure need to be finished by?* *Should it …* *How many …* *Which …*
3	Questions about the presentation	*How long should the presentation be?* *Should we …* *Does …* *Can we …*
4	Questions about the assessment	*What percentage of marks goes towards this assignment?* *How many …* *What …*

Now check the key for answers and comments on this exercise.

Understanding the purpose of a task

You will have a better chance of doing the task well if you understand *why* you have been asked to do it. You should therefore spend some time thinking about the *purpose* of the task, as well as what you think you will *learn* from it. You will find it helpful to think about:

- the aims of the module

- the learning outcomes of the module.

You can usually find the aims and learning outcomes of your module in the documentation that goes with it. Many students do not pay attention to them and miss an important opportunity to learn how to study more effectively.

Look at the aims and learning outcomes for a module in Healthcare Studies below.

For example:

Module title	Fundamentals of the Healthcare System
Module aims	To provide a critical overview of the organization and work of the British healthcare system, and to generate an awareness of the research that has been conducted into selected areas of the practice of healthcare
Module learning outcomes	To analyse the functions of a healthcare system in an industrial/ emergent post-industrial society
	To describe the conceptual, political and organizational background of the British healthcare system
	To critically evaluate the extent to which the present system meets the needs of consumers of healthcare, and, more generally, society

You should refer to the module aims and learning outcomes while doing your coursework to make sure you are focusing on the correct content. When you review your coursework, you should ask yourself if you have met the outcomes for the work you were set. For coursework in Healthcare Studies you could ask yourself the following questions.

- Have I analysed the functions of the healthcare system?

- Have I shown that I understand the purpose of the healthcare system and described how it is organized and the politics involved?

- Have I evaluated whether or not the healthcare system works well and satisfies patients and society?

- Have I found, read and referred to a wide range of sources in my coursework?

Brainstorming

Glossary

appoint
If you appoint someone to a job or official position, you choose them for it.

As already discussed in Chapter 1, brainstorming is a useful technique for coming up with ideas. The technique involves putting forward any ideas connected with the subject you are thinking about; each idea generates other ideas that can be noted down until you have a list of loosely connected ideas. You will be able to use *some* of these, but you will certainly not use all of them. After brainstorming you would normally decide which ideas you can work with and write them into your plan.

Look at how this process might work if you decided to brainstorm your ideas in the assignment below.

For example: *Design a new product for your student university shop. It should be practical in nature, bear the university logo and be affordable to students to buy as a product to use or as a souvenir.*

Brainstorming a new product for the university shop

1   If possible, make use of a flip chart or a sheet of A3 paper attached to the wall and a marker pen.

2   Appoint a secretary.

3   Agree a set time period (five minutes is about right).

4   Start making suggestions about new products; the secretary writes these down in large writing so everyone can see the ideas.

5   Group members should not comment on each other's ideas but just try to build on each suggestion.

6   At the end of the set time period, take a group rest.

7   Spend time reading quietly through all the ideas.

8   Through group discussion, cross out the least popular ideas and leave the most popular ones.

9   Agree on the best idea from the remaining popular ones. Try to include everybody's opinion and adopt one idea that everybody is happy with.

Exercise 2

Brainstorm the task on page 31 on your own for five minutes, noting down everything that comes to mind. When you finish, think about the possibilities of each suggestion. Then you will be ready to make a final list of good ideas.

It might be helpful if you attach a piece of paper to the wall so you can brainstorm and make notes standing up. This helps many people to think more freely. Keep brainstorming for the full amount of time. Ideas build slowly, one idea leading to another; good ideas often come at the end of the process.

Now check the key for comments on this exercise.

Making a schedule for your group work

Glossary

deadline
A deadline is a time or date before which a particular task must be finished or a particular thing must be done.

collate
When you collate pieces of information, you gather them all together and examine them.

It is always important to finish your tasks on time. In order to do this, you have to understand what tasks need to be done, who is going to do them and when they need to be finished. One way of doing this is by using a Gantt chart. This can show the following information in graphic form: a list of sub-tasks, the date when they have to be done and who is responsible for doing them.

Look at the group assignment below.

For example: *Conduct a survey among city centre shoppers to discover the strength of popular support for a new indoor shopping mall in the city centre. Present your findings in a written report of 2,500 words by the deadline given on the front of this sheet.*

The first stage is to work together to write a list of sub-tasks for the assignment. For the group assignment above you might produce a list of sub-tasks.

1 Write questions for your group to ask the shoppers.

2 Design a survey feedback sheet to record answers.

3 Carry out the survey in the city centre.

4 Collate all the answers, in other words, put them all together and get some clear data.

Glossary

methodology
A methodology is a system of methods and principles for doing something, for example for carrying out research.

5 Draft the different parts of the report: an introduction, a methodology section, a results section, a discussion section and a conclusion.

6 Add some charts to give a visual representation of the answers.

7 Review and edit the report.

8 Write a final draft of the report.

9 Print out, bind and submit the report.

The next stage is to allocate group members for the sub-tasks.

For example:

Task	Group member
Write the questionnaire.	Everyone
Design the survey feedback sheet.	Adnan and Gisele
Type up, print out and distribute the feedback sheet.	Roberta
Carry out the survey.	Everyone
Collate data.	Taka
Write a draft of each part of the report.	Introduction: Adnan and Gisele Methodology: Taka Results: Roberta Discussion: All Conclusion: All
Add charts.	Taka
Review and edit the report.	All
Prepare the final draft of the report.	Roberta
Print, bind and submit the report.	Adnan and Gisele

After allocating roles, you need to add the time when the sub-tasks should be done, as shown in the table on page 34.

Group Work

Task	Group member	To be completed on
Write the questionnaire.	Everyone	Monday, 1/10/12
Design the survey feedback sheet.	Adnan and Gisele	Tuesday, 2/10/12
Type up, print out and distribute the feedback survey sheet.	Roberta	Tuesday, 2/10/12
Carry out the survey.	Everyone	Wednesday, 3/10/12
Collate data.	Taka	Thursday, 4/10/12
Write a draft of each part of the report.	Introduction: Adnan and Gisele Methodology: Taka Results: Roberta Discussion: All Conclusion: All	Friday, 5/10/12 Saturday, 6/10/12 Sunday, 7/10/12 Monday, 8/10/12 Monday, 8/10/12
Add charts.	Taka	Tuesday, 9/10/12
Review and edit the report.	All	Wednesday, 10/10/12
Complete the final draft of the report.	Roberta	Thursday, 11/10/12
Print, bind and submit the report.	Adnan and Gisele	Friday, 12/10/12

Finally, you can put all this information into a chart format (similar to a Gantt chart).

For example:

Task	Group member	Date (October)											
		1st	2nd	3rd	4th	5th	6th	7th	8th	9th	10th	11th	12th
Write questionnaire	Everyone	✗											
Design survey feedback sheet	Adnan & Gisele		✗										
Type up, print and distribute	Roberta		✗										
Carry out survey	Everyone			✗									
Collate data	Taka				✗								
Draft introduction	Adnan & Gisele					✗							
Draft methodology section	Taka						✗						
Draft results section	Roberta							✗					
Draft discussion section	Everyone								✗				
Draft conclusion	Everyone								✗				
Add charts	Taka									✗			
Review and edit report	Everyone										✗		
Prepare final draft of report	Roberta											✗	
Print, bind and submit report	Adnan and Gisele												✗

Exercise 3

Read about the group assignment below and fill in the table as a work chart for Sarah, Nou and Fahad. You might wish to put this into a Gantt chart using appropriate software.

Sarah, Nou and Fahad have five days to complete a group work assignment: *making a video of their university campus as a guide to new students*. On the afternoon of the fifth day, they are going to show the video to the class and give a presentation justifying and explaining their video. They met on Monday morning to plan their week's work and decided the following:

- On Monday afternoon they will split up and each group member will research and visit the locations they have chosen to focus on.

- On Tuesday morning Sarah and Nou will team up and video Sarah's locations while Fahad writes the script for the introductory part of the video. In the afternoon, when Sarah and Nou video Nou's locations, Fahad will research locations for the opening shots of the video.

- On Wednesday morning Sarah and Fahad will video the opening shots for the film and in the afternoon they will video the locations that Fahad chose. In the afternoon Nou will start preparing the digital presentation to use on Friday.

- On Thursday the whole group will edit the film in the morning, and in the afternoon they will work on the details of the presentation.

- On Friday morning the group will practise their presentation so they can give it to the class on Friday afternoon, when they also show their film.

		Mon a.m.	Mon p.m.	Tue a.m.	Tue p.m.	Wed a.m.	Wed p.m.	Thur a.m.	Thur p.m.	Fri a.m.	Fri p.m.

Now check the key for answers to this exercise.

Setting goals and objectives

Your group might find it useful to have a *list* of goals that they are working towards. Drawing up such a list of goals can be a useful team-building exercise. The goals can be referred to on a regular basis to make sure your group is on track.

You should always set SMART goals, as shown below.

S	Specific	Your goal should be precise rather than general.
M	Measurable	Your goals should have a clear outcome that you can measure so you know if you have achieved it.
A	Achievable	Your goal should be something you are capable of doing.
R	Realistic	Your goal should be something that is possible within the restrictions of the time and resources you have available.
T	Time bound	You goal should have a clear time schedule.

Objectives are the sub-tasks that need to be done in order to fulfil your goals.

Look at a group goal and some objectives below.

For example:

Group goals and objectives

Goal: To write a 2,500-word market survey report analysing the level of support for a new indoor shopping mall in the city centre and submit it by 20th December.

Objectives

- Group to design a questionnaire together to use with shoppers
- Adnan and Gisele to design a survey feedback sheet to record shoppers' answers
- Roberta to print out and distribute the sheets to group members
- Group to carry out the survey together
- Taka to collect and analyse the data to get some clear results
- Adnan and Gisele to draft the introduction
- Taka to draft the methodology section
- Group to draft the discussion and conclusion sections together
- Taka to add charts to the report.
- Group to review and edit the report
- Roberta to type and format the report
- Adnan and Gisele to print out and bind the report for submission

---

Tip ✓ Decide whether you need a Gantt chart *as well as* a set of goals and objectives; you might find they are very similar.

Exercise 4

Read the group assignment below for students on a postgraduate course in Construction and the Built Environment.

> **For example:** *Show your understanding of good design practice by designing a new block of residential flats for the centre of this city. Your design should include drawings and a model. You will present your design to the rest of the group in a twenty-minute presentation.*

Write a list of objectives that a group might write for this task.

Now check the key for answers and comments on this exercise.

Remember

✓ Be clear about what your finished assignment should look like.

✓ Check your deadlines carefully.

✓ Break down your assignment into a list of small tasks (objectives) that need to be done.

✓ Keep an eye on your main goal at the same time as the smaller tasks.

✓ Write down goals and objectives so you can see if you are meeting them.

4 | Working collaboratively

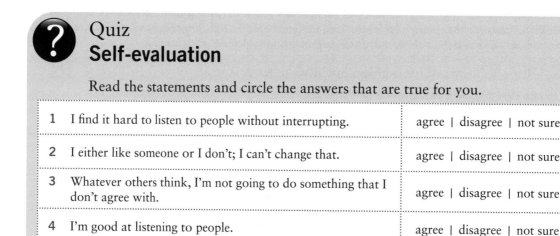

? Quiz
Self-evaluation

Read the statements and circle the answers that are true for you.

1	I find it hard to listen to people without interrupting.	agree | disagree | not sure
2	I either like someone or I don't; I can't change that.	agree | disagree | not sure
3	Whatever others think, I'm not going to do something that I don't agree with.	agree | disagree | not sure
4	I'm good at listening to people.	agree | disagree | not sure
5	I find that sometimes meetings go well and sometimes not so well. That's how things are.	agree | disagree | not sure

Now check the key for comments on this exercise.

Being an effective group member

We already know that lecturers sometimes ask you to work in groups because they want you to learn from other students and learn teamwork skills. However, this is only possible if group members *respect* each other and show this respect through their *behaviour*.

In addition to respect, there are three more important things that will help you to achieve good results when meeting together as a group:

- trust

- security

- comfort.

Exercise 1

Read about some ways that students might behave during group work. Do they make group work more or less difficult? Tick the appropriate column and then reflect on your own behaviour. Which of these things do you do? Do you need to change your behaviour in any way?

Type of behaviour	Good behaviour	Poor behaviour	Do you do this?
1 Encouraging quiet students to give their opinion			
2 Asking for help when you need it			
3 Hiding any difficulties you have			
4 Listening carefully when other students are speaking			
5 Not letting other students finish what they are saying			
6 Being rude about other people's ideas			
7 Offering an opinion on what the group should do			
8 Refusing to agree to what most of the group want			
9 Saying unkind things about other people's ideas and opinions			
10 Not being honest about things that have been said or have happened			
11 Avoiding responsibility			
12 Trying to make other students do the less popular tasks			
13 Offering to help a group member when they are finding the activity difficult			

Now check the key for answers and comments on this exercise.

Tips   ✓   Include some of this behaviour in the ground rules that you set up in Chapter 2.
　　　　　 ✓   Experiment with changes in your behaviour and monitor the reaction of others.

Having successful meetings

Meetings are a very important part of group work. During your group meetings you will check your progress, report back and make plans. But successful meetings do not happen by accident. Success depends on being organized and well prepared.

You need to think about:

- how to *prepare* for the meeting

- what will happen *during* the meeting

- what will happen *after* the meeting.

 Exercise 2

Read the list of activities below, all of which play an important role in successful meetings. Do the activities take place when *preparing* for the meeting, in other words, *before* it (B), *during* the meeting itself (D), or *after* the meeting (A)?

Activity	B / D / A
1 Deciding the date and location of the meeting	
2 Distributing an agenda for the meeting	
3 Deciding the date and location of the next meeting	
4 Reviewing progress of the group assignment	
5 Making sure the meeting room is ready with the appropriate facilities and space	
6 Discussing any difficulties the group is having	
7 Deciding on roles and responsibilities for the meeting: the secretary, the chair, etc.	
8 Discussing the last meeting and reviewing progress made against action points	
9 Making a list of action points and who is responsible for each one	
10 Writing up careful notes about the discussions and decisions that are made in meetings and distributing them to team members	

Now check the key for answers to this exercise.

Listening to others

Listening carefully to your group members is an essential part of group work during official meetings as well as more informal meetings. Some people are good at listening to others, but others need to practise their listening skills. When someone is talking and giving their point of view, you should:

- look at them to show you are paying attention

- have positive body language: facing the speaker, being open and accepting

- let them speak without stopping or interrupting them

- ask questions that enable them to provide complete views, information and answers, even if these are long

- nod your head to show you understand, even if you do not agree

- invite the speaker to continue if they hesitate

- try and reflect back what they say using phrases such as *So you think that* ....

You should not:

- say unkind things about any opinions they express

- judge what they say.

If you show you are listening to people and value their opinion, it will be easier to negotiate differences of opinion – even if you disagree with everything they are saying.

Tips
✓ Body language is an important part of listening, so show you are attentive by using eye contact.
✓ Do not feel you need to help to solve a particular issue a speaker is talking about; just show you understand it.

Exercise 3

Read the phrases below that a listener might use when someone else is speaking. Are they appropriate for encouraging a good understanding and building a good relationship between the speaker and the listener? Tick 'Yes' or 'No' and say why you think so.

Phrases	Is the phrase appropriate to show you are a good listener?		
	Yes	No	Why?
1 You shouldn't have done that!			
2 Oh, don't worry about it.			
3 How do you feel about that?			
4 I see. So you feel ..., do you?			
5 Why on earth did you do that?			
6 I think I can imagine how you feel.			
7 I think you're crazy!			
8 Hang on. There's something I want to say.			
9 Go on. I'm listening.			
10 Do you want to say more about that?			

Now check the key for answers and comments on this exercise.

Negotiating

When you are working in your group, you usually need to *discuss* issues in order to come to an agreement. This can be difficult when different group members have different ideas. Look at the group task below and read how three students negotiate a compromise by coming to a group decision on page 43.

> **For example:** *Plan a day trip for a group of school children to a local place of interest. Choose from the city zoo, an art museum or the seaside, justifying your choice of destination. Also prepare a worksheet for the children to complete during their visit.*

Gretchen:	*I think we should take them to the seaside. It's fun there. The children would have a great day out. What do the rest of you think?*
Hassan:	*But it's school. It's not just about fun. I think we should plan a trip to the art gallery.*
Katya:	*No. I disagree with both of you. I think we should think about a trip to the zoo.*
Gretchen:	*Why do you think the zoo would be a good idea, Katya?*
Katya:	*Everybody loves zoos, we all know that. It's definitely the zoo for me!*
Gretchen:	*OK. So Katya likes the zoo. Hassan, why are you so keen on the art gallery?*
Hassan:	*Well, I think we should give the children a chance to visit somewhere they wouldn't normally go to. They'd see something new. It's an opportunity to open their eyes to art. If they have a good trip, they might start to appreciate art and take an interest in it. Let's be honest, I think hardly any of them have ever been there in their lives. But most of them have been to the zoo, and they've all been to the seaside.*
Gretchen:	*That's true. I hadn't thought of it like that.*
Hassan:	*You see, when I was a kid, my uncle took me to an exhibition once and I still remember it. I still have a postcard on my bedroom wall that I bought from the gift shop.*
Katya:	*I do like art myself, but I just think the children would be bored by it.*
Hassan:	*Then we should try to make it interesting for them! It's a real challenge!*
Gretchen:	*What about if we tried to do something outside, after the gallery, so they didn't spend all day indoors?*
Katya:	*I wonder if we could stop at the park on the way back from the gallery. They could have an ice cream.*
Gretchen:	*Yes, how about that park with the butterfly garden? It's a bit like the zoo?*
Katya:	*And we know they like zoos!*
Hassan:	*So they would get the best of both worlds!*

Group Work

In this negotiation the group was successful in arriving at an agreement. Successful negotiations are achieved by:

- remembering that the goal is to *reach an agreement*

- avoiding any attempt to 'win' the negotiation

- giving individual opinions

- supporting each opinion with good reasoning

- *listening* to others

- being open-minded about alternatives

- making compromises.

Exercise 4

Find useful phrases for negotiating in Gretchen, Hassan and Katya's conversation and write them in the correct place in the table below.

Phrases for:	Phrases used:
1 giving opinions	
2 asking other people's opinions	
3 disagreeing	
4 questioning opinions	
5 giving a reason for an opinion	
6 agreeing with somebody	
7 offering a solution	
8 showing understanding of another's point	
9 showing a suggestion is new or unusual	
10 making suggestions	

Now check the key for answers and comments on this exercise.

How groups develop

As time goes by, your group will change. You will get to know each other better and understand how each member thinks and works. This will help you to become more effective as a group and more able to tackle problems. Research shows that groups often go through distinct phases as time passes: *Forming, Storming, Norming, Performing* and *Adjourning*. If you can understand these phases, it will help you to understand why things happen the way they do.

Exercise 5

Look at the five phases of group development. Match the phases 1–5 with their descriptions a–e.

Phase 1: Forming	a	In this phase, group members are comfortable with each other. They are more able to work together, negotiate and compromise and make group decisions.
Phase 2: Storming	b	This is the final phase of the group. After finishing the task they were set, the team breaks up and reflects on the experience that they had.
Phase 3: Norming	c	In this phase, group members are on their best behaviour because they want to make a good impression on each other. There is reliance on the lecturer for direction. Not much is achieved. The team members act quite independently from each other.
Phase 4: Performing	d	In this phase, the group is a high performing team. They identify themselves as a team, support each other in tasks and achieve their objectives efficiently.
Phase 5: Adjourning	e	In this phase, the group members start to open up and realize that there are many different ideas and opinions in the group. There may well be some competition between group members to find out who is more dominant, and the group will be struggling to find ways to work together.

Now check the key for answers to this exercise.

Remember

✓ Successful groups work collaboratively and come to group decisions.

✓ You will usually have to compromise during group work.

✓ You might sometimes have to go along with decisions you do not like.

✓ Give your opinion and reasons for it during negotiations.

✓ Listen carefully to other students and be prepared to change your mind.

✓ Your group will change as time goes by, so do not worry too much if things are difficult at first.

5 | How different people learn and study

Aims ✓ understand the impact of learning styles on group work

✓ recognize the link between personality types and team roles.

✓ understand the role of cultural differences

Aims

? Quiz
Self-evaluation

Read the statements and circle the answers that are true for you.

1	People are basically the same despite superficial differences in language and culture.	agree | disagree | not sure
2	Some people just don't try hard enough: anyone can do anything if they put their mind to it.	agree | disagree | not sure
3	I don't like to plan everything out in detail before starting work. I just go with what feels the right thing to do.	agree | disagree | not sure
4	I am a very practical person: I like to think about things that are here and now.	agree | disagree | not sure
5	We should take on a team role that is appropriate to our personality.	agree | disagree | not sure

Now check the key for comments on this exercise.

The importance of learning styles and personality types

Glossary

superficial
If you describe something such as an action, feeling or relationship as superficial, you mean it includes only the simplest and most obvious aspects of that thing.

Over the last 40 years, there has been a lot of research and discussion in the West about how different students prefer to learn and study. If this idea of different learning styles is new to you, you will find it particularly useful to think about how *you* like to study and what makes a good learning situation for *you*. If you are already familiar with the concept, you can still learn from looking at these ideas again.

You will be more successful in working as part of a group if you are aware of your learning style and the learning style of your team members. By understanding learning styles you can:

Glossary

learning style
Learning styles are the different methods that students use to learn and their particular approaches to studying.

- learn and study more efficiently using a style that suits you

- understand why other people want to do things differently from you

- take on an appropriate role in the group

- take responsibility for appropriate tasks in your group.

Watchers, doers, feelers and thinkers

Glossary

formulate
If you formulate something such as a plan or proposal, you invent it, thinking about the details carefully.

According to one model of learning styles, there is a four-stage process that we go through when we learn something.

1 First we experience it.

2 Then we think about and reflect on what we experienced.

3 Then we formulate some ideas about what we have experienced.

4 Then we act and test out our ideas.

Individual learners have different abilities. You might be:

- a **Watcher** who likes to experience things by *watching* other people

- a **Doer** who likes to experience things by *doing it for yourself*

- a **Thinker** who *thinks carefully and rationally* about a task

- a **Feeler** who *responds emotionally* to a task.

These learning types represent opposites as shown in the diagram below. Most people are somewhere between the four extremes.

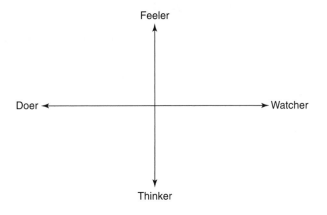

Exercise 1

Where would you place yourself on the lines in the diagram above? Decide whether you are more of a *Doer* than a *Watcher*, and if you are more of a *Feeler* than a *Thinker*. Put a cross on each line according to where you think you are.

Then read descriptions of four learner types: Diverging learners, Accommodating learners, Assimilating learners and Converging learners. Is one of these an accurate description of you? If not, do the exercise again and decide if the model really does not work for you or whether you have misinterpreted it.

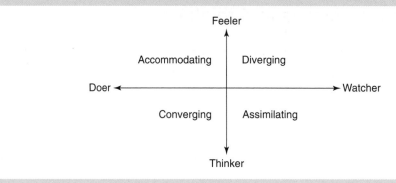

Now check the key for comments on this exercise.

Diverging learners

These learners are *Feelers* and *Watchers*. This means they tend to watch what other people do and collect a lot of information. They are good at thinking up new ideas and brainstorming. *Feelers* and *Watchers* tend to be emotional and creative. *Diverging learners* are usually good at group work and sensitive to what is going on around them, as well as thoughtful about other people's feelings.

Accommodating learners

These learners are *Feelers* and *Doers*. *Doers* are practical people who like to get on with things in their own way without worrying whether it is the correct or best way; they just do things in the way that feels right for them. *Accommodating learners* (or *Accommodators*) are useful to have around when no one is sure what to do because they will just go ahead and do it. These people may let other people do the thinking as they prefer to be active rather than sitting around and analysing things. *Accommodators* enjoy working in teams to solve problems.

Assimilating learners

These learners are *Watchers* and *Thinkers*. They are ideas people. One of their strengths is the ability to take a lot of complex information and present it in a simple, easy-to-understand way. They are less interested in other people than they are in ideas, theories and logical explanations. *Assimilators* tend to make good scientists because they are interested in systems and categories and like to take time to work things out properly.

Converging learners

These learners are *Doers* and *Thinkers* and, like *Assimilators*, are less interested in other people than they are in technical things such as computers and different computer programmes. It is likely that they enjoy solving problems using technology, but not by discussing things in depth with other people. *Convergers* are practical people and are likely to have interesting new suggestions about how to do things.

Source: Excerpts and diagrams from Kolb, D.A. (1984): Experiential learning: experience as the source of learning and development

Learning styles and group work

You will find that other students in your group learn and study in different ways from you. It is very important to understand this and take it into account. You should:

- tolerate the different ways that other students want to do things

- explain why you want to do something in a different way

- understand that you need to present information in such a way that it is accessible to students with a range of learning styles.

Read the commentary in the table on page 50 on the different learning styles that have been discussed. This will help you to relate the learning styles to how they affect group work.

Divergers, Accommodators, Assimilators and Convergers		
Type of learner	Comments	Don't forget
Divergers Feelers and Watchers	You should do well in your group learning. Your strength is in seeing issues from different viewpoints and making suggestions.	Other students in your group might think you do not do enough because you do not take the lead and are happy to watch other people do things.
Accommodators Doers and Feelers	Your strength is in getting on and using your initiative to do tasks. You respond well to group work and are happy to try different things to solve problems.	Other group members might think you go off too quickly without having a clear plan or without analysing things carefully enough. You might need to slow down a little and explain to others why you are doing things.
Assimilators Watchers and Thinkers	Your strength is that you are logical and rational and you can explain exactly why things should be done in a certain way. You might find it a bit difficult to work in groups because you are less interested in people than others in the group.	The others in your group might think you are a bit uncommunicative. Find time to talk to your group members so they can understand who you are and what you think.
Convergers Doers and Thinkers	Your strengths are in using technology and solving technical problems and difficulties.	Other group members might think you are a bit distant. Take the time to interact with them or they might think that you do not like them.

Personality types

A lot of research has been done into personality types and how these can also affect groups of people working together. The general conclusion is that your personality type will have a *considerable* effect on how you behave when you are part of a team.

One model of personality concentrates on four important areas, namely whether you:

- are an introvert or an extrovert

- are interested in the 'here and now' or the possible

- think logically or are more emotional

- plan things carefully or like to make things up as you go along

Exercise 2

Read the descriptions of the four personality types on pages 52–53. Choose which one best describes your personality and answer the questions below.

1 Are you an Introvert (I) or an Extrovert (E)?

   Write **I** or **E**.   _____

2 Are you a Sensing (S) or an Intuition (N) type?

   Write **S** or **N**.   _____

3 Are you a Thinking (T) or a Feeling (F) type?

   Write **T** or **F**.   _____

4 Are you a Judgement (J) or a Perception (P) type?

   Write **J** or **P**.   _____

Write your four letters together to give you your personality type. You will be one of the following:

ISTJ, ISTP, ESTP, ESTJ, ISFJ, ISFP, ESFP, ESFJ, INJF, INFP, ENFP, ENFJ, INTJ, INTP, ENTP, ENTJ.

Your personality type will be used in Exercise 4 to help you to relate to the role that you can play in your team.

Now check the key for comments on this exercise.

- **Are you an introvert or an extrovert?**

  Introverts are people who are more interested in themselves and their own thoughts and feelings than in other people, directing their energy inwards to themselves. Introverts observe and analyse a lot, and when they relate to other people they do so within small groups or one-to-one. Introverts are stimulated when working alone, and tend to be quieter and less likely to display their feelings than extroverts. They often relax when on their own rather than in company.

  Extroverts like to work with other people rather than on their own; their focus is on the outside world and on action rather than on their own private inner world. Extroverts probably find it easier than introverts to open up to others and discuss their personal feelings. Extroverts are more likely to relax by socialising with other people than by being on their own.

- **Are you interested in the 'here and now' or the 'possible'?**

  Here and now (Sensing type)
  You are somebody who likes to rely on facts and figures that you know are true, and you like information that is reliable and concrete. You are practical and if you have to do something, you will do it based on reliable information in an ordered way. You pay attention to detail and think it is important to follow correct procedures.

  The possible (Intuition)

  You rely on your own feeling or instinct about how to do things. You often spend time using your imagination and thinking up new ideas. If you have to do something, it is likely that you will do it the way that feels right to you. You are interested in thinking about the different possible things that might happen.

■ Do you think logically or are you more emotional?

Think logically (Thinking type)
You make decisions based on good logical reasoning. You will take time to analyse things from an objective standpoint and you will be consistent in your decisions. You are careful about relying on your emotions because you know that they can be **irrational**. You are prepared to be unpopular in your decision making if you know the decision is fair and right.

More emotional (Feeling type)
You tend to rely on your emotions when you need to make a decision about something. You do not want to carefully weigh up the evidence or analysis, but prefer to use your own intuition of what is right or wrong and carefully consider the effect of your decision on other people.

■ Do you plan things carefully or do you like to make them up as you go along?

Plan things carefully (Judgement type)
You like to control things by planning carefully. You are very organized and have everything laid out carefully – nothing is left to chance. You make sure you know what is needed before starting on a project and think things through carefully. You are likely to be ambitious and like to achieve your goals.

Make things up as you go along (Perception type)
You are relaxed in your approach to what is going to happen in the future. You enjoy not knowing exactly what the future will bring and like to leave the door open to unexpected opportunities. You are adaptable and flexible and respond well to new developments.

Team roles

The Type Mapping System™ suggests that there are eight different roles which describe the most important things people do when they work in teams. The eight roles described in the table below will help you to understand how people behave during group work. The roles explain the contributions that different types of people bring to the team.

Role in the team	Description of role
Clarifying	You like to make things clear. You listen to other people, ask questions and categorize everything carefully. You have a good eye for detail and can explain information and ideas clearly.
Analysing	You like to explain things: your analysis explains what is happening and brings structure to ideas. You fully understand any difficulties that are going on and look at evidence for an explanation.
Innovating	You have a vivid imagination and use it to investigate the world from different viewpoints. You produce new and surprising solutions to problems and think in the long term.
Campaigning	You have very strong ideas, typically ideas that are backed by beliefs or values. You will focus on strong ideas because you think they are the most important.
Harmonizing	You like to bring the separate group members together into a strong team. You work to make people feel valued and motivated. You solve problems between other people and create a good working atmosphere.
Exploring	You look for new ways of doing things as well as new ideas. You are always exploring new possibilities and experimenting with ways to improve things.
Conducting	You are the one who organizes the *way* things are done. You concentrate on setting up the roles in a team and make sure that everybody has clearly defined responsibilities and that they fulfil these responsibilities.
Activating	You act immediately in response to situations. In a group environment, you also encourage other people to respond to things. You want to have an immediate impact on the situation, to have clear goals and see quick results.

Source: Excerpts from Type Mapping™ System by Roy Childs and Steve Myers. MTR-I™ and ITPQ™ are the trademarks of S.P. Myers. TDI® is the registered trademark of Team Focus Limited.

The value of these descriptions is that they relate to roles and activities that play an important part in group work. If these activities are not carried out by any of the team members, your team is likely to underperform.

The activities also provide a sequence in which you can work through your group work task.

1   Clarifying: making sure the task is clear and collecting information to tackle it

2   Analysing: examining the task in detail

3   Innovating: coming up with different possible ways to work on the task

4   Campaigning: evaluating the different ideas and choosing the best ones

5   Harmonizing: thinking about the people involved and how to motivate them

6   Exploring: investigating the effectiveness of ideas to see if they are going to work

7   Conducting: planning who will do what and when and with what resources

8   Activating: taking action to complete the task

Exercise 3

Think about the team roles above. Which ones do you think most closely resemble your personality when you take part in group work?

Now check the key for comments on this exercise.

Personality types and team roles

You can link your personality type to the team roles suggested on page 54. The table below shows the team role that your personality is likely to adopt in group work.

Personality type	Team role
ISTJ and ISFJ	Clarifying
ISTP and INTP	Analysing
INTJ and INFJ	Innovating
ISFP and INFP	Campaigning
ESFJ and ENFJ	Harmonising
ENTP and ENFP	Exploring
ESTJ and ENTJ	Conducting
ESFP and ESTP	Activating

Tips   ✓   Knowledge of personality types and team roles can help you to understand what is happening during group work and why people behave the way they do.

   ✓   Use the information about personality types to help you to choose the most appropriate role for you in your team and to take on appropriate responsibilities and tasks.

Tips

Exercise 4

Think about what you have read about learning styles and personality types. Make notes under each heading. In the final column summarize what skills you will bring to your group.

My contribution to the team			
My learning style according to the Watchers/Doers, Thinkers/Feelers model	My personality type according to I or E, S or N, T or F, J or P	The role that I am likely to adopt in my group	What I will contribute to the team

Now check the key for comments on this exercise.

When you find yourself working in a group, it would be useful for each group member to complete a similar form to the one in Exercise 4 so you can share your findings in a rewarding group discussion.

Essential roles in good teams

Other research suggests that if a team is going to be successful, it has to have team members who fulfil specific important roles. These roles are not 'responsibility roles'; in other words, they are not seen as indicating what responsibility a group member should take on, but are roles that anybody, whatever post they are in, might take up. If nobody in your group is taking up that role, you might find your group does not achieve its potential.

There are nine roles (see the table below), so members might need to play more than one of these roles in small groups.

Role	Explanation of the role
Plant	You are creative, imaginative and free-thinking. You generate ideas and solve difficult problems. On the other hand, you can sometimes ignore incidental issues and are sometimes too preoccupied to communicate effectively.
Resource investigator	You are outgoing, enthusiastic and communicative. You explore opportunities and develop contacts. However, you can sometimes be over-optimistic, and you can lose interest once your initial enthusiasm has passed.
Co-ordinator	You are mature, confident and can identify talent. You are good at clarifying goals and you delegate effectively. You can sometimes be seen as manipulative, and sometimes offload your own share of the work on others.
Shaper	You are challenging and dynamic and thrive on pressure. You have the drive and courage to overcome obstacles. However, you may be prone to provocation and can offend other people's feelings.
Monitor evaluator	You are sober, strategic and discerning. You are able to see all the options and judge accurately. On the other hand, you may sometimes lack drive and the ability to inspire others. You can also be overly critical.
Team worker	You are co-operative, perceptive and diplomatic. You are able to listen to others and avoid friction. However, you can be indecisive in critical situations and tend to avoid confrontations.
Implementer	You are practical, reliable and efficient. You are able to turn ideas into actions, and organize work that needs to be done. On the other hand, you can be rather inflexible and slow to respond to new possibilities.
Completer finisher	You are painstaking and conscientious. You search out errors and tend to polish and perfect the things you undertake. You may be inclined to worry unduly and can be reluctant to delegate.
Specialist	You are single-minded, self-starting and dedicated. You provide the knowledge and skills that others lack. However, you may only contribute on a narrow front and tend to dwell on technicalities.

For more information on what to do when things get hard, see Chapter 7.

Tips ✓ Refer to the roles on page 57 at the end of group meetings and group work sessions.
✓ Identify how the team members behave in certain roles. If some roles are not being covered, you may find group work difficult.

Cultural differences in learning

Glossary

distinction
If you make a distinction you say two things are different.

People from different cultures speak different languages, eat different food and behave differently in many aspects of their lives. So students who come from different cultures will also behave differently; in other words, they will have different ways of learning, studying and socialising, whether in school, college or university.

One distinction that is sometimes made in cultures is between *collectivism* and *individualism*. Collectivist cultures are those in which people consider themselves to be primarily members of a larger group; in such cultures, the interests of the group are put first. In individualistic cultures people consider themselves to be individuals first and put the interests of the group second.

The table below shows other widely accepted beliefs about collectivist and individualistic cultures.

	Collectivist cultures	Individualistic cultures
Regions/Countries	Asia, Middle East, Africa, South and Central America	USA, Western Europe, Australia
How parents want their children to behave	To be well-behaved, respectful, loyal to the family	To be high achievers, fulfilling their potential, happy
The general aim of education	To improve the student's social status	To improve the student's earning power in the future
What teachers are expected to do	To teach knowledge/facts	To teach students to think for themselves, have opinions
How students are expected to behave in class	Not to ask the teacher many questions Not to speak out much	To ask the teacher a lot of questions and challenge the teacher To speak out often in front of the class
Area of education often focused on	Facts	Skills

Exercise 5

How do you think students from collectivist and individualistic cultures might approach group work differently? Make notes.

	From collectivist cultures	From individualistic cultures
1 During group discussions		
2 During whole class discussions		
3 If there is a problem about something in the group		

Now check the key for answers and comments on this exercise.

Remember

✓ Different people learn and study in different ways, so you should respect students who do things differently from you.

✓ Be patient with students who are reluctant to speak out; understand why they are not used to speaking in front of a large group.

✓ Lecturers give you group work so you can learn to work with people who are different from you.

✓ Understand that you must be prepared to compromise during group work as there is usually no one correct way to do something.

6 | Monitoring progress

Aims ✓ review your own performance ✓ review your goals
✓ review the team's performance
✓ give and receive feedback on peer performance

Aims

Quiz
Self-evaluation

Read the statements and circle the answers that are true for you.

1	I don't need to worry about my own performance; I always perform well.	agree | disagree | not sure
2	It's a matter of luck whether you have an effective team.	agree | disagree | not sure
3	I don't feel comfortable commenting on the performance of other students in my group.	agree | disagree | not sure
4	I don't want to keep stopping to see where the group has got to; I just want to get on and do things.	agree | disagree | not sure
5	Once given a task it is important to see it through to the end.	agree | disagree | not sure

Now check the key for comments on this exercise.

Reviewing your own performance

As you progress through your group assignments, it is helpful to take some time to think about the performance of your group. You can think about how *you* are performing, how the *individuals* in your group are performing and how the *team* is performing. Reflecting on these things helps you to see if you can make any improvements in your teamwork.

Before you begin to evaluate other people, it is probably a good idea to think about how you have been performing yourself. You should consider:

- your behaviour towards your group members

- your achievement of the tasks you are responsible for

- your performance in meetings

- your attitude.

Exercise 1

Complete the self-evaluation form below in relation to any group work you are currently doing, group work you have done in the past, or how you imagine yourself working in groups.

Self-evaluation form	Never				Always
	1	2	3	4	5
1 I attend group meetings.	1	2	3	4	5
2 I am well prepared for group meetings.	1	2	3	4	5
3 I listen to my group members and show respect for what they are saying.	1	2	3	4	5
4 I contribute to meetings by giving my ideas.	1	2	3	4	5
5 I offer my group members help when they need it.	1	2	3	4	5
6 I complete the tasks I have been assigned or I am on track with the tasks I have been assigned.	1	2	3	4	5
7 I am open-minded and make compromises where necessary.	1	2	3	4	5
8 I am approachable when my team members need to contact me and ask me something.	1	2	3	4	5

I have reflected on my performance and I could improve it by:

1 _____

2 _____

3 _____

4 _____

Now check the key for comments on this exercise.

Tips ✓ Create your own self-evaluation form to reflect your own group rules.

✓ Review your achievements against a Gantt chart that you can create with your group.

✓ Have a sharing session in your group where you each share your individual feedback. This will strengthen your group and build trust within it.

Reviewing the performance of your team

Glossary

peer
Your peers are the people who have the same age as you or have the same status as you.

The most important performance for you to review is that of your group. Even if you do not review your individual performance or the performance of your peers, it is important to consider how you are working *together*; this will probably have the biggest impact on the final mark you get for your group assignment.

When you reflect on the performance of your group, remember that a good team can achieve more than the individuals within it. You should evaluate how your group works as a team rather than the work each individual member does away from the group.

Exercise 2

A group evaluation form is a good way to review the performance of your team. Look at the example form on page 63 and think about the information it contains. If this was your group evaluation form, what changes would you want to make to improve your group work? Make notes in the final section of the form (reproduced below) to show the things you would want to change.

What changes do we want to make to improve our group work?

1 _____

2 _____

3 _____

4 _____

5 _____

Now check the key for comments on this exercise.

For example:

Group evaluation form			
	Yes	Don't know	Don't think so
1 We have regular group meetings.	✓		
2 We know what we are going to do when we meet as a group.			✓
3 Group members are keen to offer each other help when it is needed.			✓
4 Group members feel comfortable asking for help.		✓	
5 When we have group discussions, group members feel comfortable giving their opinions.	✓		
6 Everybody contributes when there is a group discussion.		✓	
7 Group members are well suited to their group roles.			✓
8 The individual members understand their roles and responsibilities properly and address them.		✓	
9 The decisions are made by the whole group collectively and through compromise.			✓
10 We trust each other.	✓		
11 Everybody's skills and strengths are exploited to the full.			✓
12 Every person feels a valued member of the group.		✓	
13 We regularly review our progress using our Gantt chart.			✓
14 All the group members appear to be committed to the group goals.	✓		
15 We are on track with our tasks.	✓		
16 We review our team goals regularly.			✓
17 We have the skills that we need within our group to complete our tasks and achieve our goals.	✓		
18 We have the resources that we need to complete our tasks and achieve our goals.		✓	

What changes do we want to make to improve our group work?

1 _____

2 _____

Giving and receiving feedback on peer performance

It might be useful for your team to evaluate each other's individual performance. If your group is working well together and there is trust between group members, this can be a rewarding experience. However, you should be careful and *sensitive* about making comments about other group members' performances. If there are some members of the group who are insecure and there is a lack of trust within the group, you might decide this activity is not appropriate. In this case, group feedback may be a safer level for you to work at.

The following activity is a way in which groups can give anonymous feedback to members of the group and enable them to reflect on their performance in the light of their peers' comments.

1 Create enough feedback sheets so there is one for each group member.

2 Sit in a circle and start to fill in a feedback sheet for yourself, including your name, your role and your responsibilities.

3 Pass on the feedback sheet to another student. Each student gives some feedback to the team member whose name is at the top of the sheet by putting a tick in the relevant column for each desirable quality. They can also add comments in the comment box in the bottom part of the form.

4 Pass on the feedback sheets until everybody has had a chance to work on everybody's form.

5 Students should take away their sheets from the group meeting and think carefully about the comments. Students should complete the section at the bottom of the sheet.

6 At the next group meeting, students can share the comments they made at the bottom of the sheet.

Exercise 3

Look at the peer evaluation form below. If this was a feedback form that your group members had completed about you, what reflective comments would you want to make? Read the comments and make notes.

Reflection on my peers' comments:

1 _____

2 _____

3 _____

4 _____

5 _____

Peer evaluation form			
Student name: Taka Kato			
Role in group: IT specialist			
Main responsibilities:	Peer reviewers' feedback		
	Always	Sometimes	Never
Attends group meetings	✓✓✓	✓	
Is well prepared for group meetings	✓✓	✓✓✓	
Listens to the group members and shows respect for what they say	✓✓✓✓✓		
Contributes to meetings by giving ideas	✓	✓✓✓	✓
Offers group members help when they need it		✓✓✓✓	✓
Is open-minded to suggestions and is prepared to compromise	✓✓✓	✓✓	
Has completed the tasks assigned or is on track with them	✓✓	✓✓✓	
Is committed to the group goals	✓✓✓	✓✓	

Peer reviewers' comments
Things I would like to thank this team member for:

It's easy to meet up with him and discuss things outside group meetings.
He is cooperative and friendly.

Things I would like my team member to think about:

I don't think he always comes up with enough ideas.
He could be a bit more proactive.

Reflection on my peers' comments:

1 _____

Now check the key for comments on this exercise.

Reviewing group goals

It is important to review the goals you have set your group and check your progress against them. If not, you might find that your goals have shifted, and each member has a different idea of what they are. You might need to:

- change the goals if circumstances have changed

- change your strategy if you are not meeting your goals

- change your team members' roles if the current responsibilities are not working

- ask someone outside the team for help.

In order to review your group goals, you must first *have* some group goals (see Chapter 3). You can use the goal review form on page 67 to review your goals as a group during a group discussion.

1   Distribute the form to members of the team; make sure everybody has a copy of the group's goals that you prepared earlier in your group work process.

2   Individual members should prepare for the group discussion by thinking about the group's goals individually before meeting as a group.

3   When you hold your group discussion, share your opinions about how successfully your group is achieving its goals. Make notes in the columns as you discuss.

4   Pay particular attention to the final column. Note down your ideas and opinions about the changes to group practices you need to make in order to achieve your goals.

Exercise 4

Read the goal review form on page 67. It has been completed for a group working on this task from Chapter 3.

Example: *Show your understanding of good design practice by designing a new block of residential flats for the centre of this city. Your design should include drawings and a model. You will present your design to the rest of the group in a twenty minute presentation.*

Think about what might have happened to the assignment if the group had not reviewed their goals.

Now check the key for comments on this exercise.

Goal review form			
Goal	Still appropriate?	Achieved it or on track?	If not, why not? What needs to happen to get on track? Is there a new goal?
Goal 1: Carry out research into good design practice and its important features.	Yes	Yes, research completed and list of features to incorporate in building drawn up.	
Goal 2: Carry out research into the nature of the city centre, its needs and current style of architecture.	Yes	Yes, task divided up; have pooled research; have clear idea of what new building needs to look/be like and who it is for.	
Goal 3: Design an appropriate building for the city centre taking your research into account.	Yes	No	Goals 1 and 2 took a long time, so now behind schedule. Until Goal 3 done, cannot move ahead with Goals 4 and 5. Need to plan a large amount of time to complete Goal 3 together.
Goal 4: Make a drawing of the building using an appropriate software package.	Yes	No	We need to allocate responsibilities to different team members for these tasks. Can then start work on these as soon as Goal 3 is completed.
Goal 5: Make a model of the building.	Yes	No	
Goal 6: Prepare a presentation to explain and justify the design.	Yes	Yes	Yes, have time to think about these goals nearer the time.
Goal 7: Deliver the presentation.	Yes	Yes	

Tip ✓ You need to review smaller tasks on a regular basis. Always bring your Gantt chart to meetings and make sure everyone is up to date on their tasks.

Remember

✓ Always reflect on your group's performance in order to improve it, as well as your own and other members' performance in the group.

✓ Be prepared to change roles if you need to.

✓ Be sensitive if you give feedback to peers.

✓ Review your progress regularly so that you find out in time when things are not on track.

7 | When things get hard

Aims ✓ recognize and identify problems within groups
✓ understand how to solve problems
✓ understand group dynamics
✓ deal with difficult group members
✓ understand when to seek support

Aims

? Quiz
Self-evaluation

Read the statements and circle the answers that are true for you.

1	It's better to ignore problems than face them; they might just go away.	agree | disagree | not sure
2	An argument should be avoided at all costs.	agree | disagree | not sure
3	Some people just aren't good at group work.	agree | disagree | not sure
4	If there are weak members of the group, I should work on my own so I can get a higher mark.	agree | disagree | not sure
5	If I take a problem to my lecturer, they will think I have failed in my group work.	agree | disagree | not sure

Now check the key for comments on this exercise.

Recognizing and identifying problems

It is not unusual for groups of students to run into difficulties when they are working together. It is therefore a good idea to look out for difficulties and deal with them early and openly, rather than hoping they will fix themselves. Remember that one of the reasons lecturers give you group work is so that you learn to *solve* difficulties that come up during teamwork. Always remember that you will get a good mark in your group work assignment if you can show that your group recognized and solved group problems.

Watch out for signs that your group might be having difficulties, for example:

- One or more members of the group regularly miss meetings.

- You cannot easily contact one or more members of the group.

- Your group meetings are very short.

- Your group meetings are tense rather than relaxed.

- Some of your group members seem unhappy.

- Some group members do not contribute to group meetings.

- The group is not on track with its tasks and goals.

Exercise 1

Read about some typical group problems 1–9 and make notes on the possible cause(s) of each problem.

Problem
1 Some students do not say anything during group meetings.
2 The group meetings are dominated by one or two students who talk all the time.
3 One or more students regularly miss meetings.
4 One or more students do not do their work adequately.
5 It is hard to contact one or more of the group members.
6 You find that your group cannot agree on what to do.
7 One or more members of the group want everyone to do things their way and will not compromise.
8 Group meetings are too quiet and few members have anything to say.
9 Group members are not sure what their task comprises.

Now check the key for answers and comments on this exercise.

Solving group problems

If your group has difficulties, you will need to use appropriate *strategies* to try to overcome them. The strategies you use will depend on the type of problem and how serious it is.

Exercise 2

Match the group issues 1–6 with the strategies for dealing with them a–f.

Issue	Suggested strategy
1 Some students do not say anything during the meeting.	**a** This requires a serious group meeting in which the situation is opened up and discussed. If group work turns into a power struggle, you will face serious challenges and you might not achieve anything. Your group will need to negotiate and compromise. It may take one brave group member to break the deadlock.
2 Some students are not doing their fair share of the work.	**b** Review the group role responsibilities as somebody should be responsible for preparing the agenda. At the end of a meeting, agree what you will discuss at the next meeting. Let people know what will be discussed before the meeting so they can prepare things to say.
3 Some students do not compromise and want everything done their way.	**c** You need some practice in negotiating. Read Chapter 4 again.
4 Group meetings are too quiet and few members have anything to say.	**d** ■ Make sure that students understand their tasks by reviewing them at the end of each group meeting. Make sure the tasks are well defined. ■ Use a group task agreement form to highlight important tasks so that students commit to their task publicly.
5 You cannot agree on what to do because everyone has different ideas.	**e** ■ You need to find a way of making students aware of this aspect of their personality. If they continue in this way, they will not learn teamwork skills. ■ You may want to use a ground rules reminder form. This strategy should only be used when the group work situation is very poor and you think you will need to ask for help from outside your group.
6 The group breaks into smaller **factions** who do not get on with each other and nothing is agreed.	**f** Give the students advance warning about the content of the discussion so everyone can prepare their comments in advance. Also: ■ The group chair should actively nominate group members to contribute. ■ Make sure students feel that their comments are valued by listening carefully and showing appreciation for them.

Now check the key for answers to this exercise.

One way of dealing with group work difficulties is by video recording a group session and watching it together afterwards. This can be a powerful way of getting group members to become aware of their behaviour. It might be used during difficult times to raise the awareness of a particular group member, or it might be used as a matter of course during a progress review.

You can only video a session if all the group members accept the idea. You will also need to agree what to do with the recording after you have watched it. If you agree to use video, it can be helpful to use a form to evaluate your group dynamics and individual behaviour, such as the one in Exercise 3.

Exercise 3

Read the group dynamics evaluation form that has been completed by a group member after watching a video of their group work. Tick the appropriate column.

Group dynamics evaluation form

As you watch the recording of your group work session, tick the appropriate column of the table for each of the seven aspects of behaviour. Add comments of your own.

	True	False	Don't know	Comments
1 One member of the group did most of the talking.				*Faiz always seems rather talkative, but on the video you can see he lets others participate.*
2 All members of the group contributed to the discussion.				*Jane is a bit quiet, but she does make some good points. On the other hand, Alora is quite noisy but doesn't really say anything about the topic we are discussing.*
3 Everybody was polite and respectful to everybody else.				*I think Faiz sometimes sounds a bit rude though he doesn't mean to be. I think it's a cultural thing and we have to understand it's normal for him to be a bit 'lively'. He certainly tries hard to be friendly and helpful.*
4 The decisions were arrived at through negotiation.				*This is difficult to evaluate. There seems to be discussion, but the suggestion from Raul is the one everyone seems to agree to.*
5 Everybody did their fair share of the work.				*It's clear that a couple of members of the group hadn't done enough background reading even though they tried to show they had.*
6 Everybody was present and on time for the meeting.				*I'd forgotten that Jane went a bit early and that Didier came in late while we were sorting out the room.*

Now check the key for answers and comments on this exercise.

This kind of reflective work on your group dynamics demonstrates what your lecturers hope you will learn from group work.

Dealing with difficult group members

Glossary

cope
If you cope with a problem or task, you deal with it successfully.

inadequacy
If someone has feelings of inadequacy, they feel that they do not have the qualities and abilities necessary to do something or cope with life in general.

ridicule
If you ridicule someone or ridicule their ideas or beliefs, you make fun of them in an unkind way.

There may be some group members who are particularly difficult to work with. Remembering the stages of group formation (Forming, Storming, Norming and Performing) will help you to understand *why* students may be difficult to work with at different stages of the group work process.

Group work can be quite stressful and hard for some students to cope with; individual students may react in different ways. Here are some reactions that students might have.

- feelings of inadequacy leading to an avoidance of tasks

- fear that weak students might pull down the group mark, resulting in them doing most of the work and taking all the decisions

- feeling left out by the rest of the group, resulting in them being more forceful than they might usually be

- uncertainty about the appropriate behaviour that is expected in group work

All of the above might result in an aggressive or uncooperative response that could be misunderstood. Group members who are difficult to work with may:

- avoid tasks or not do their tasks satisfactorily

- miss meetings

- refuse to go along with group decisions or to find a compromise

- not let people talk in meetings

- ridicule the ideas of others in the group

- criticize the work of other students.

If you have a group member who you or your group finds difficult to work with, there are a number of stages you can work through.

Stage 1: Do some group monitoring progress tasks (see Chapter 6). This may raise awareness and deal with the problem. You can use a task agreement form if one team member is not working hard enough.

In this form each member's task will be noted down and nobody will feel victimised. The first four columns should be completed at the end of a meeting when the tasks are being allocated. The final column should be completed after the tasks are finished so that group members can give comments on how well they feel the task was completed.

For example:

Task agreement form				
Group member	Task	Complete by	Agreed and signed by	Group feedback on the task
Faiz	Research current use of solar panels	10 Feb	Faiz Ahmed Faiz	Not enough detail or examples to show impact of solar panels in UK market
Juan	Talk to manufacturer of hybrid panels	10 Feb	Juan dos Santos	Good summary of research. Need details of person interviewed, position, etc.

Stage 2: If the problem continues, your group needs to make the individual aware of the group's feelings about their behaviour. This can first be done informally by speaking with the person.

Stage 3: If the problem continues, your group needs to formally notify the person that their behaviour is not acceptable to the rest of the group. This can only be done if there is consensus in the rest of the group; it needs to be done sensitively and supportively. You could do this by officially reminding your group member about the group's ground rules (see page 74).

For example:

Ground rule reminder

To group member: Axel Hertz

In order to improve our group work, please remember the following ground rules:

1 All work needs to be shown to the group before it is submitted.

2 Any problems with completing the task have to be discussed with the group before submission.

3 All discussions should be carried out in a polite and constructive manner.

Please let us know how we can support you in our group work.

Signed by your group members:

Juan dos Santos   Faiz Ahmed Faiz   Gisele Fournier

Stage 4: If problems persist, you may need to go outside the group for help.

Seeking support

If your group has serious difficulties, you might need to seek support outside your group. You might hesitate before doing this as you might expect to be penalised for failing in your group work. But if your group is failing and you have done everything you can, it is a good idea to keep your tutor or lecturer informed of the problems.

You should be aware that your tutor or lecturer will be expecting:

- that there may be group difficulties, so they will not be surprised or upset to hear about them

- to be told about serious group problems such as bullying or failure to do any work

- to be told how you have already tried to solve problems in your group

- to be given precise information about difficulties rather than general complaints about group members.

Bear in mind that lecturers are busy people, so they should only be approached after you have tried to solve the problems for yourselves and if you think the problems are serious enough for such an intervention. Also bear in mind that they will not want to hear *all* the details of any disagreement.

There may be other support services available within your university that you can make use of. They may have useful advice about solving group work problems. Services include:

- the language support service

- the learning development service

- the academic support service

- the university counselling service.

Support services are set up by the university to provide help to students. The people involved are always ready to listen to problems that any student might face. Sometimes it only takes one conversation to clarify a situation or deal with a misunderstanding.

Remember

✓ Problems usually get worse if they are not dealt with.

✓ In Western countries people usually want to deal openly with difficulties.

✓ In Western countries people think that an argument might be a good thing because it can clear the air.

✓ You might have to go outside the group if you have serious problems.

8 | Presenting in a group

Aims ✓ assess group presentations   ✓ practise a group presentation
       ✓ plan a group presentation   ✓ deliver a group presentation

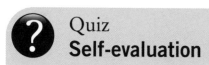

Quiz
Self-evaluation

Read the statements and circle the answers that are true for you.

1	There isn't much difference between a group presentation and an individual presentation.	agree | disagree | not sure
2	Group presentations aren't fair because everyone gets the same mark.	agree | disagree | not sure
3	Weak students have an advantage in a group presentation as the other students can help them.	agree | disagree | not sure
4	We can use colloquial language during a group presentation to show we are relaxed.	agree | disagree | not sure
5	Students aren't usually interested in other students' presentations in class.	agree | disagree | not sure
6	A presentation is a formal occasion and needs to be taken seriously.	agree | disagree | not sure

Now check the key for comments on this exercise.

The purpose of a group presentation

Presentations are a popular form of assessment in English-speaking universities. When you give a presentation, marks are usually awarded for:

- content

- structure

- presentation skills and use of visual aids

- language skills.

Glossary

cue card
Cue cards are cards with notes written on them to remind a speaker of what they want to say during a presentation or speech.

academic register
Academic register of a piece of speech or writing is the level and style of language that is used in a university context.

intonation
Your intonation is the way your voice rises and falls as you speak.

delivery
You talk about someone's delivery when you are referring to the way they give a speech or lecture.

Some lecturers might combine these elements and then add more criteria, but they will all be looking for similar things. When watching a student presentation, a lecturer will be thinking about the points below.

Content
- Is there evidence of research?
- Are references used and sources reworked, and made relevant to the presentation?
- Is there evidence of learning?
- Is there evidence of critical thinking and analysis?
- Is a good argument presented?
- Are reasonable conclusions drawn?

Structure
- Is there an introduction that opens up the topic and gives the background for the presentation?
- Are there a number of identifiable main points?
- Is there a conclusion that sums up the presentation and leaves the audience with a clear message?

Presentation skills/Use of visual aids
- Is there good use of body language?
- Does the speaker have good eye contact with the audience?
- Does the speaker engage the audience?
- Is the speaker comfortable using notes or cue cards, not script?
- Is the digital presentation well designed without too much text on each slide?

Language skills
- Is there good use of signposting language to guide the listener through the presentation?
- Does the speaker make good use of academic register?
- Is the speaker easy to understand?
- Is there appropriate use of intonation and stress?
- Is there good use of specific vocabulary?
- Do grammatical mistakes get in the way of meaning?

When you do a group presentation, there are a number of other things you need to think about. First of all, you should think about *why* you have been asked to give a group presentation rather than an individual presentation. Your lecturer wants to see:

- that the group has worked closely together

- that you have learned some group work and teamwork skills during the process

- that you have all contributed to the research, the planning and the delivery of the presentation.

Group Work

Your lecturer will also want to see one cohesive presentation rather than a series of separate presentations by the individual members of the group. To get good marks in your shared presentation, you need to *demonstrate* that you have worked together as a group. Linked to this, you need to demonstrate that you are *developing* your teamwork skills.

Exercise 1

Read about some strategies that groups might use in their group presentation. Tick the appropriate column to show whether you think it is good or bad practice.

Strategy	Good practice	Bad practice
1 Divide up the presentation into different sections at the beginning of the presentation process and allocate group members to prepare the different sections.		
2 Let the stronger student(s) do most of the talking in the presentation.		
3 Let a dominant student take control of the planning and delivery of the presentation.		
4 Practise the presentation on your own.		
5 Practise the presentation together.		
6 Refer to other parts of the presentation and other group members when you are giving your own part of the presentation.		
7 Introduce yourselves as a group at the start of the presentation.		
8 Make a list of responsibilities for the presentation and allocate them to members of the group.		
9 Take it in turns to do things such as operate the slides and talk during the presentation.		
10 Refer to any problems you had in the preparation stage during the actual presentation.		
11 Divide the presentation into many small sections, with a different speaker for each, so that each student speaks two or three times.		

Now check the key for answers and comments on this exercise.

Tip ✓ Be careful not to work separately on the preparation too early in the process. When you try to put the parts together, it might seem like several separate ones.

Planning your group presentation

As with any group task, you will need to work closely together to plan your presentation. When you begin planning, you need to consider:

- your objectives: the *purpose* of the presentation

- your audience: how much they already *know* about the topic and what *interest* they have in it

- the guidelines you have been given: how long the presentation will last, where you will give it and what format it will be in.

These considerations will guide you in the *preparation* of your presentation. You should start with a group discussion to make sure you understand the key points before planning in detail. You could complete a form to help prompt your thinking.

For example:

Presentation guidance form	
Objectives	
1 What is the aim of the presentation?	To explore the benefits of hybrid solar panels that can generate electricity and heat water simultaneously.
Audience	
2 Who is the audience?	Second-year undergraduate students in Mechanical Engineering and other students who might have seen the advertising and be interested in the topic.
3 How much do they know already about the topic?	The Mechanical Engineering students will know about the principles of thermodynamics, and everybody will know about the government drive for renewable energy.
4 What do they want to know?	Whether combining two technologies will have the advantages that are claimed.
5 What do we want to tell them?	A background of the two technologies with their advantages and disadvantages, and how combining them is more than just the sum of the two parts.
Guidelines	
6 How many presenters will there be?	A group of three or four students.
7 How long should it last?	20 minutes.
8 How many slides should there be?	20
9 Other points	This is of real interest to students as it shows how it is possible to apply simple principles to create new and innovative products that benefit society.

Tips ✓ Complete the presentation guidance form and give a copy to every group member.
✓ Bring out the form every time you work on the presentation so you can refer to it and to make sure that you are on track.
✓ Remember your audience! If your only reason for the presentation is to get a good mark, it will probably be uninteresting. If you think of your presentation as an opportunity to inform, explain, discuss and explore a topic for your audience, you are more likely to give an *effective* presentation.

Tips

Preparing an effective group presentation involves a number of tasks. It not only involves deciding what tasks you have to do, but also what *order* you need to do them in.

Exercise 2

Your group presentation task list could include the points below. Put them in the correct order. The first one has been done for you.

Group presentation task list

_____ Make a digital presentation/a poster/visual aids/hand-outs.

_____ Practise the presentation before you give it.

_____ Prepare the room for the presentation.

___1___ Decide on the general topic.

_____ Write cue cards for use during the presentation.

_____ Prepare the introduction.

_____ Prepare each of the main points with a focus and a clear argument.

_____ Prepare the conclusion.

_____ Have a discussion about the objectives, audience and guidelines for the presentation.

_____ Research the content.

_____ Choose three or four points to focus on as the main parts of the presentation.

Now check the key for answers and comments on this exercise.

You also need to think about which preparatory tasks should be done individually and which ones should be done as a group. As in all group work activities, the allocation of tasks is an important part of working efficiently and effectively.

Exercise 3

Read about the tasks that need to be done when preparing for a group presentation. Write G if you think they should be done as a group or I if you think they should be done by an individual.

Task	G / I
1 Make a decision about the topic of the presentation.	
2 Research the content.	
3 Prepare the introduction.	
4 Make a digital presentation.	
5 Practise the presentation before giving it.	
6 Write cue cards.	
7 Prepare each of the main points with a focus and a clear argument.	
8 Prepare the room for the presentation.	
9 Research the content.	
10 Choose the three or four main points of the presentation.	

Now check the key for answers and comments on this exercise.

Practising your group presentation

You should practise your presentation before you give it. You might decide it is a good idea to practise your individual part on your own, but you also need to practise the presentation as a group. The practice times should be agreed well in advance so that everyone is present. It should be far enough in advance of the real presentation so that there is still time to work on it if a problem emerges.

You should practise the presentation as if you were actually giving it. For example, if you are using cue cards in your real presentation, you should use cue cards in your practice. You do not know which parts will be difficult until you practise. Group members can watch each other and make *constructive* comments on how to improve:

- the content of the presentation
- the structure of the presentation
- your presentation skills
- your language skills.

After you have practised your presentation, you should have a discussion about any improvements you need to make.

Tips
- ✓ Make and watch a video of your practice presentation so you can go over what you need to improve more than once.
- ✓ When you have finished preparing and practising your presentation, try to relax. Do not try to make last minute changes; these are more likely to cause problems than result in improvement because of the disruption they cause.

Delivering your presentation

Glossary

arise
If a situation or problem arises, it begins to exist or people begin to become aware of it.

Your group presentation should be an example of what a group can achieve when it works well together. You have already looked at ways this can be achieved. The following points, grouped in five specific areas, incorporate them in the context of the actual delivery.

1   Things to consider:

- introducing yourselves as a team at the start of the presentation

- ways of working as a team to deliver the presentation so that each of you has clear responsibilities, for example, speaking, working the slides, giving hand-outs

- helping a group member who needs support

- referring to things that other group members have said or will say

- referring to some aspects of group work that arose during the preparation of your presentation

2   Things the presenter is always advised to do both in group and individual presentations:

- use notes or cue cards rather than a script

- maintain eye contact with the audience for most of the presentation

- deliver the presentation to everyone in the audience, including the other students, not just the lecturer

- be enthusiastic about the presentation you are giving, and engage the audience in it

- ask the audience for questions at the end of the presentation

3 Things that lecturers in English-speaking universities expect to see:

- that you are well-prepared and have spent time researching and thinking about your presentation

- evidence of reflection and analysis in the points you make in the presentation

4 You will lose marks if you:

- do not look at the audience when you talk

- read your script word for word

- cannot explain something which you have had time to prepare for

- deliver content that you have taken from somewhere else without reworking/paraphrasing it (this is plagiarism and is a serious academic offence).

5 Things you are generally *not* expected to do:

- wear smart clothes for your presentation: you can if you wish, but you will not get better marks (and it might look strange if some of your group dress up but others do not)

- learn your presentation off by heart: you can use notes and cue cards to help you to talk as a presentation is not a memory test (lecturers like to see you well-prepared, but also *thinking on your feet*)

Tips
✓ It is better to ask your lecturer about something than to worry about it on your own.
✓ Your lecturer or tutor will be happy to answer questions you have about your presentation before you give it. If you have a question you would like to ask, other students probably have the same question.

Remember

✓ Keep in close contact with your group members during the preparation process; otherwise your presentation might appear disjointed.

✓ Try to show how you worked as a group to prepare your presentation.

✓ Practise your presentation as a group before you actually give it.

✓ Show that you are working as a group when you *deliver* your presentation.

9 | Writing in a group

Aims ✓ plan your group writing task ✓ proofread the final draft
✓ revise drafts and give peer feedback ✓ carry out reflective writing

Aims

Quiz
Self-evaluation

Read the statements and circle the answers that are true for you.

1	There's no such thing as group writing; you just divide up the work and do your part alone and put everything together at the end.	agree | disagree | not sure
2	I prefer to just write rather than spend time on planning.	agree | disagree | not sure
3	I tend to stay up late before a deadline as I usually leave work to the last minute.	agree | disagree | not sure
4	I know that I make mistakes when I write, but I can't seem to find them for myself.	agree | disagree | not sure
5	Reflective writing sounds easy. You just talk about what you did!	agree | disagree | not sure

Now check the key for comments on this exercise.

Planning your group writing task

It is very important to start your group writing assignment *together*. The first thing is to have a group discussion to make sure you all agree on the answers to questions, for example:

- What is the aim of the writing assignment?

- Who is the audience and what do they expect to read about?

- What are the central themes and arguments?

- How will these central themes and arguments be organized?

Glossary

framework
A framework is a particular set of rules, ideas or beliefs which you use in order to deal with problems or decide what to do.

capacity
The capacity of something such as a factory or airport is the quantity of things it can produce or deal with using the equipment or resources that are available.

expand
If something such as an organization or service expands, it becomes larger.

It is a good idea to write a plan, or framework, for your assignment *before* you divide up the work and allocate it to group members. This way each group member will be providing input to all parts of the assignment, and it will be more likely to fit together as a whole. The framework for your piece of writing should include each section of the assignment, the main ideas you intend to talk about, some of the sources you will be using and the word count.

Before looking at a writing framework, read the following group writing assignment and think about the questions that follow.

> **For example:** *Write a report explaining the current debate around UK airport capacity and the different options available to expand that capacity.*

- Do you know anything about this topic already?

- What kind of sources do you think you would use for your research?

- What structure might you use for your report?

Read the discussion about how a group might start to plan this group writing assignment.

Ahmed:	*OK. British airport capacity! What do we know about that?*
Jodie:	*Well, I saw a politician on the news the other day talking about the possibility of building a new airport – because Heathrow isn't big enough.*
Gerhard:	*And I remember seeing some signs near Heathrow saying 'No third runway'.*
Ahmed:	*So the problem is that the UK needs more airports. The title says 'explaining the current debate'. So do we know what the main arguments are in the debate?*
Gerhard:	*Not yet! I think we should do some research, first. We've got that reading list to go through. We need to find out about all the options for increasing airport capacity. We've got two already – expanding Heathrow and building a whole new airport. Then we can discuss the arguments and explore the points for and against each option.*
Jodie:	*Let's make some notes. First of all, we'll need an introduction. We want to introduce the topic so we'll have to give some background.*
Ahmed:	*And we need to give a justification for the report and give the structure as well ...*

Group Work

Now look at a possible writing framework for the assignment.

For example:

Writing assignment framework			
Section	Purpose and main ideas	Some sources to be referred to (more to be added later)	Word count
Section 1: Introduction	■ Introduce topic ■ Introduce aims ■ Give some background ■ Justify report ■ Describe structure of report		500
Section 2: Importance of airport capacity	■ Explain why airport capacity is important for economic growth ■ Discuss importance and impacts of hub airports	*Economic impacts of hub airports,* British Chamber of Commerce, July 2009	1,000
Section 3: Solution 1, expand Heathrow	Discuss advantages and disadvantages of expanding capacity at Heathrow by building more runways	http://hub.heathrowairport.com http://www.priorityheathrow.com *Connecting for Growth,* Frontier Economics	1,000
Section 4: Solution 2, build a new airport	Discuss possibility of building new airport in Thames Estuary plus advantages and disadvantages of idea	*Thames Estuary Options,* Daily Record, 2012	1,000
Section 5: Solution 3, expand other airports	Discuss possibilities of expanding other airports – Stansted, Gatwick	*The importance of aviation infrastructure to sustainable economic growth,* FTI, 2011	500
Section 6: Conclusion	Review problem, highlight most feasible options and state urgency of finding solution		300

Once you have a framework, you are ready to allocate writing responsibilities to different group members. You should then agree a date when you will produce the first draft of the section you are responsible for.

Tip ✓ Do not try to change the framework of your writing on your own. If you think the framework needs changing, you should have a group meeting to agree this.

Revising drafts

Clearly, this involves two processes: revising *your own* work and *peer revision* of the work of the other group members. It is a good idea to revise your own work before showing it to other members of your group. It is therefore particularly important to follow a clear schedule when writing in groups. If you rush your writing and finish just before meeting, you will not have had time to make revisions.

Exercise 1

When you are writing in a group, it is a good idea to follow clear steps. Put the steps below in the correct order.

_____ Proofread your work for grammar, spelling and punctuation mistakes.

_____ Write your first draft.

_____ Share what you have written with your group.

_____ Have a break.

_____ Give feedback to group members on the content of their writing.

_____ Revise what you have written.

_____ Revise your writing in the light of feedback from group members.

Now check the key for answers to this exercise.

If you have a break of about a day between writing your first draft and revising it, you have a much better chance of reading it with a fresh mind and eye, and spotting things you might want to change.

In the first stages of revision, you should be focusing on the *overall content* of the writing. You need not worry too much about mistakes in grammar and punctuation at this point. Instead, you should be asking yourself questions such as the following (these apply to both your own work and the work of your peers).

1   Is the meaning clear?

2   Are the main points well expressed?

3   Are the arguments clear and logical?

4   Is there a clear progression from one idea to another?

5   Is there use of references to outside sources (if appropriate)?

6   Is there critical analysis of ideas leading to a conclusion?

Tip ✓ Be sensitive when you give feedback to your group members on their writing. If you are critical of someone who has made a big effort, they might take offence.

Here are some useful phrases for giving feedback to group members.

Giving feedback

That's great. I think it's really good.

I like this part where you say that ... But I think this part here could be improved.

Can I make some suggestions? Why don't you say more about ...?

It might be an idea to focus more on ...

Do you think you could add a bit more on ...?

Didn't we decide you would cover ...?

I like what you've done so far, but it would be even better if you added/changed/moved ...

Notice that each comment begins either in a positive way or uses a polite phrase before going on to make a suggestion for change.

Proofreading

Proofreading is the final stage of checking your writing when you are happy with the overall content. When you proofread, you look for small mistakes in grammar, spelling, punctuation and style. It can be difficult to proofread your own work as you are less likely to spot the mistakes you have made. Proofreading what others have written in your group is a good opportunity to practise this very important skill, which you can then apply to your own work.

While you are proofreading, it can be helpful to look for particular mistakes instead of just hoping you will find errors as you read. The table on pages 89–90 shows some common grammar mistakes that international students often make in their writing.

Common grammar mistakes		
Mistake	Example	Tips
Articles: *the / a*	*Heathrow Airport is busiest airport in Europe.* Correct version: *Heathrow Airport is **the** busiest airport in Europe*	Check all singular nouns. If they are countable, they need an article or determiner such as *some* or a *lot of*.
Singular/ Plural	*Hub airports bring important benefit to their regions.* Correct version: *Hub airports bring important **benefits** to their regions.*	Check nouns: do you mean one in particular, or more than one?
Subject–verb agreement	*Smith (2012) believe that the UK is missing out on trade with emerging markets because of its restricted airport capacity.* Correct version: *Smith (2012) **believes** that the UK is missing out on trade with emerging markets because of its restricted airport capacity.*	Look at the subject and verb: do they agree? Check for third person *s* in the present tense.
Tense	*Last year 30 million passengers use Heathrow Airport.* Correct version: *Last year 30 million passengers **used** Heathrow Airport.*	Look at the time period you are talking about. Is it the past, present or future?
Word form	*A new runway could improve the efficient of Heathrow.* Correct version: *A new runway could improve the **efficiency** of Heathrow.*	Check the word form: do you need a noun, verb, adjective or adverb?

Group Work

Mistake	Example	Tips
-ing form	~~Expand~~ Heathrow would be unpopular with the residents in the area. **Correct version:** *Expanding* Heathrow would be unpopular with residents in the area.	You can make a noun phrase with an *-ing* form. *Expanding Heathrow* is an example of a noun phrase.
Active / Passive verb	A fifth terminal ~~added~~ to Heathrow recently despite much local resistance. **Correct version:** A fifth terminal **was added** to Heathrow recently despite much local resistance.	Is the sentence active or passive voice? If passive, use *be* + past participle.
Prepositions	Further detailed figures can be found ~~on~~ the appendix. **Correct version:** Further detailed figures can be found **in** the appendix.	The rules for using prepositions are complex. Always check prepositions, and use a dictionary if in doubt.

Exercise 2

The text below contains examples of the types of mistake identified above. Underline the mistakes and write the text correctly.

Many students come from all over world to study in UK. There is many reasons for this, but they usually say that have a British degree will help them to find good job in their country later on. Although some foreigner students have great time when they study abroad, others find it more difficult.

One of the main problems in study in an English-speaking university is different academic culture. In Western universities students expected to critical analyse material, whereas in some cultures the main emphasis is on learning fact.

Another difficulty that student may face is on the area of the language. Students which have English as a second language have to learn how to express himself in academic and colloquial situation. This might not be easy as it is not always possible to meet native English speakers to practise English with.

Study in UK can be hard work, but it is also very reward. Although experience can be difficult, student often look back at their university days with happy.

Now check the key for answers to this exercise.

Reflective writing

Reflective writing is a popular form of assessment in English-speaking universities. Teachers want students to think about something that has happened during their study and discuss what they have learned from it. Your lecturers think that this reflection is a powerful part of the learning process.

Here are some reflective writing assignments.

> **For example:** *Watch the video of the presentation you gave earlier. Write a 500-word reflective account of what you have learned from preparing, delivering and watching your presentation.*

> **For example:** *Reflect on your experience of working in your group. Write 1,000 words about what you have learned from your group work experience.*

The most important things to remember about reflective writing are that you should:

- be open and honest about any problems you experienced

- *analyse* what happened; don't just *describe* what happened

- say *what you learned* and say *how you would do things differently* if you had to do them again.

Reflective writing is used to *demonstrate* that you can analyse your experiences and show what you have learned from them. Your lecturers believe that an experience not reflected on is not a very useful experience. So when reflecting on a piece of work, you need to *show* your lecturer that you are able to produce a better piece of work in the future. Some of the most important things you experience might be the mistakes and problems you had. It is particularly important to learn from these.

If possible, let a little time pass before writing your reflection. This will help you to be more objective about it. However, you might find it is a good idea to mull things over during this time, before sitting down and thinking seriously.

When you work on your reflective writing, it will help you to think of these questions.

1   What skills did you learn as you worked through your assignment?

2   What subject knowledge did you learn?

3   What skills do you now realize you need to improve?

Group Work

Glossary

anticipate
If you anticipate an event, you realize in advance that it will happen.

reference
A reference is a word, phrase, or idea which comes from something such as a book, poem, or play, and which you use when making a point about something.

overcome
If you overcome a problem or a feeling, you successfully deal with it and control it.

hindsight
Hindsight is the ability to understand and realize something about an event after it has happened, although you did not understand or realize it at the time.

4   What problems arose that you had not anticipated?

5   How did you tackle any problems that arose?

6   How would you do things differently if you did a similar assignment in the future?

7   Was your problem solving effective? How could it have been more effective?

8   What strengths and weaknesses have you noticed about yourself, and what can you do to address the weaknesses?

9   What theory from outside references can you bring in to support what you say you have learned?

10 What conclusions can you draw from the whole assignment experience?

Here are some useful phrases for reflective writing.

Reflective writing

One of the most challenging aspects of the assignment was …

One of the most difficult things to overcome was …

If I did a similar assignment in the future, I would certainly …

I had not predicted …

I did not expect … to happen.

I/We tried to overcome the problem by …

With hindsight, it would have been a good idea to …

I have improved my … skills.

I found I was able to …

I realize that I need to work on …

I learned that …

For more information on learning from your group work experience, see Chapter 12.

Tip   ✓   Reflective writing is different from other academic writing because it is written in the first person using 'I' but it still needs to be written in an academic style.

Tip

Exercise 3

Read this extract from a piece of reflective writing on a group work assignment. Identify and underline the points that demonstrate an ability to reflect. These points will result in more marks being awarded for the writing.

> *There was one part of our Environmental Science group work which I found very challenging at the time. We had all finished our field work, and we had to upload our results onto the shared drive by the end of the week (we had set Friday 5.00 p.m. as the deadline) so that we could start to analyse them over the weekend. One of the group members did not meet the deadline and did not upload her results, so we could not go on to the next stage of the project.*
>
> *She had been late with her part of the work a couple of times before, and she had promised to get her work done by the agreed time. When I realized that she had missed the deadline and still hadn't posted anything by Saturday, I sent her an email telling her that it was not good enough and that she had let everyone down. She called me almost immediately on my mobile, and we had an argument over the phone. She had an excuse about her mother being ill and having to go home and look after her but I didn't believe her at the time. I said some things that I regretted later, and the phone call really upset me.*
>
> *I made some notes about what had happened later that day. Looking back at those notes, I can see why I reacted the way I did, but now that I have more background information about my group member, I also understand why she behaved the way she did. I need to think about why I acted so aggressively towards her missing the deadline and also why I took the argument so personally. There will inevitably be disagreements in professional life, and I need to find a way of managing them well. I also need to think about how I can show I am not very happy about something without upsetting the other person too much.*

Now check the key for answers and comments on this exercise.

Remember

✓ Make sure you plan your writing thoroughly before you divide up the work for different group members.

✓ Stick to your writing plan to make sure your writing links together properly.

✓ Revise your writing for content before you proofread it for grammar and spelling.

✓ Be sensitive about how you give feedback to group members on their writing.

✓ Show what you have learned in reflective writing rather than describing what you did.

10 | Study groups

Aims ✓ understand the role of a study group
✓ form a study group

✓ identify different purposes for study groups: lectures, reading, presentations, writing, seminars and exams

Aims

? Quiz
Self-evaluation

Read the statements and circle the answers that are true for you.

1	I get bored studying on my own; I'd rather do it with other people.	agree | disagree | not sure
2	I would like to study with other people, but my friends are on different courses.	agree | disagree | not sure
3	When I am with my friends, we chat about other things – not work.	agree | disagree | not sure
4	I prefer to study on my own than with other students.	agree | disagree | not sure
5	I don't want to practise my presentation in front of other students – it's too embarrassing.	agree | disagree | not sure
6	I think that individual work has to be done individually, so I always do it on my own.	agree | disagree | not sure

Now check the key for comments on this exercise.

What is a study group?

A study group is a group of students who study together because they want to learn by sharing their ideas and their knowledge. As you already know, you will often be asked to work in formal groups at university for marked assessments; however, you can also form your own study groups outside this formal group work. Students form study groups because it helps them:

- to explain things to each other when one of them does not understand

- to answer each other's questions about things they might not want to ask the lecturer about

Glossary

interactive
If you describe a
group of people
or their activities
interactive,
you mean that
the people
communicate
with each other.

- to get different opinions and viewpoints on course content

- to support each other when times are hard

- to learn good study habits from each other

- to study in a more interactive and interesting way

- to motivate each other.

You can benefit from being part of a study group in many different areas of university study, for example, lectures, reading, presentations, written coursework, seminars and exams.

Forming a study group

If you are going to join a study group or start one yourself, it is a good idea to think about what sort of students you want in your group. Do you want to work with:

- the best students?

- students who you think have the same ability as you?

- students who are of mixed ability?

- students who are fun to be with?

- students who get the highest marks?

- friends?

- students who are popular?

- the hardest-working students?

Spending some time considering these questions will help you to find the right study group for you. If you have a lot of friends who are studying on the same degree programme, it might be easy to form a study group. If your friends are on different courses or if you are new to university and you do not know many other students, it may be more appropriate to use the study group to actually make new friends.

Exercise 1

Read about some strategies you could use to look for other students to form a study group. Which strategies do you like best? Make notes about the advantages and disadvantages of each strategy.

Strategy	Advantages	Disadvantages
1 Approach other students individually before or after a lecture to ask them about starting a study group.		
2 Speak to a lecturer and ask for permission to make an announcement to the whole class about starting a group.		
3 Put a notice up on a noticeboard asking students to contact you.		
4 Give out slips of paper to students asking them to contact you about setting up a group.		
5 Send an email to all students studying your module.		

Now check the key for answers and comments on this exercise.

Tip ✓ If you write a notice or a hand-out asking for interest in forming a study group, it is a good idea to spend time on the design and wording of your document. When students read your notice, they will gain an impression of you, and this will influence whether or not they contact you.

When you have assembled a study group, it is a good idea to agree on some guidelines about how it will be organized. Agreeing on guidelines for your study group is a good way to make sure you all have the same expectations.

Exercise 2

What kind of guidelines should a study group adopt? Read the *Dos* and the *Don'ts* for study groups below. Tick the appropriate column.

	Guideline	Do	Don't
1	Let students who regularly miss lectures use the study group to catch up on material.		
2	Ensure that members bring the correct study equipment to meetings.		
3	Allow students to be late or miss meetings.		
4	Arrange a regular time and place for meetings.		
5	Spend a large amount of time during meetings socialising.		
6	Insist that students notify the other members of the group if they cannot attend a meeting.		
7	Allow students who have not done the reading to copy notes from other members of the group.		
8	Choose a leader to organize and run each meeting.		
9	Plan what you are going to do in your next study meeting at the end of your current meeting.		
10	Make a list of things that students have to do in preparation for the next study group meeting.		

Now check the key for answers and comments on this exercise.

Study groups for lectures

Students in study groups can work together to make sure that they make the most of their lecture programme at university. They can collaborate *before*, *during* or *after* lectures to make sure that they are learning as much as possible.

Exercise 3

Read about some useful activities that groups of students can engage in. Write B if the activity takes place before the lecture, D if it takes place during the lecture or A if it takes place after the lecture.

Activity	B / D / A
1 Write some questions that you expect to be answered.	
2 Sit together, take notes and look at each other's notes.	
3 Record the lecturer speaking.	
4 Listen to the recording that was made of the lecture and discuss it.	
5 Prepare some specialist vocabulary that you expect to come up during the lecture.	
6 Sit down together and tell each other the main points from the lecture.	
7 Do some reading before the lecture and share your ideas on what you have read.	
8 Look at the lecture title and the module documentation so you know what to expect from the lecture.	

Now check the key for answers and comments on this exercise.

Tip ✓ Remember that a study group is *in addition* to your usual work: it is not a replacement for attending lectures and seminars or a way of avoiding doing your own individual work.

Study groups for reading

When you are studying at university, there is a lot of background reading to do. You will be given a reading list for each module you do, and you will probably be surprised at how much there is to read. By working in a study group, students can support each other, but they need to follow good study practices and be careful not to do the work for each other.

Exercise 4

Read about some ways that students might work together to manage their background reading. Are they good or bad study practices? Make notes explaining why/why not.

Ways that students help each other	Good or bad practice? Why/Why not?
1 All students read the core text separately and then come together to check their understanding of the key points.	
2 Students divide up the core text. Each student reads a different part. They then tell the other students what their part was about.	
3 Students make notes about core texts and then look at each other's notes.	
4 Students share any *extra* suggested reading and then come together to tell each other the main points of what they read.	
5 Students share the extra suggested reading, make notes and then copy each other's notes.	

Now check the key for answers and comments on this exercise.

Study groups for presentations

Your study group can be a useful support when you have a presentation to give. It is important that *you* do the research, planning and preparation yourself, but your study group can play a big role in helping you to *practise* your presentation. Shortly before you give your actual presentation, you can give it to your study group and ask them for feedback.

Exercise 5

Think about practising your presentation in front of your study group. What kind of feedback would you want them to give you? Which areas would you want them to comment on? You will need to think about this in advance or you might get the wrong kind of feedback.

Look at some questions you could ask your study group to answer as they watch your practice presentation. Add as many more questions of your own as you can.

Questions on my presentation

Do I have good body language?

Is my presentation interesting?

Do you think there is enough analysis of the topic?

_____

_____

_____

_____

Now check the key for answers and comments on this exercise.

Tips ✓ Practise your presentation long enough in advance so you can make some changes if you need to after feedback.

✓ Encourage your study group to ask you some questions at the end of your presentation so you get some practice thinking on your feet.

Study groups for writing

Glossary

collusion
Collusion is secret or illegal cooperation, especially between countries or organizations.

Students can support each other in their writing tasks, but it is very important that in individual work you do not collaborate too closely and hand in the same piece of work. This is collusion, a serious academic offence, and the penalties for this can be severe. However, there are still ways that you can support each other in your writing. You can:

- discuss ideas and possible resources

- read each other's work and comment on the content

- read each other's work and comment on grammar, punctuation and spelling mistakes.

Glossary

offence
An offence is a crime that breaks a particular law and requires a particular punishment.

penalty
A penalty is a punishment that someone is given for doing something that is against the law or rule.

adequately
If something is done adequately, it is done well enough to be used or accepted.

As mentioned in Exercise 5, it is important to say what sort of feedback you want from your study group; for example, it can be frustrating to get feedback on your grammar if you were looking for feedback on the quality of your written argument. Here are some examples of questions you might give to a study group member to get some feedback on your writing.

- Have I answered the question adequately?

- Is the purpose of the text clear?

- Is the structure of the text clear and logical?

- Is there good paragraphing?

- Have I quoted enough sources in my work?

- Do you think the bibliography shows enough background reading and research?

- Are there any serious grammar mistakes?

- Should I provide any more background information in the appendices?

Tips

✓ Do not expect members of your study group to do too much to help you during individual writing work: it is *your work* and if you try to rely on other students, they are likely to resent it.

✓ You might want to share individual written work with just one member of your study group rather than with the larger group.

Study groups for seminars

Seminars can be difficult situations for international students. In seminars you have to:

- give your opinion on a topic

- justify your opinion

- ask for other people's opinions

- agree and disagree with other people.

You might also have to:

- talk about background reading you have done

- talk about research you are involved in

- present an assignment you have been given.

The most useful way a study group can support each other with regard to seminars is by providing an environment where students can practise their speaking skills and improve their confidence in taking part in discussions.

Exercise 6

Read about some activities that students could do in study groups to improve their discussion skills and build their confidence. Tick the ones that would work well for you. Put a question mark for those that would need to be adapted to make them more suitable for you, and make notes about the modifications you would make.

Activities	✓ / ?	How it could be modified
1 Sit down with your study group and get the others to quiz you about the last lecture you attended together.		
2 Prepare and give a talk to your study group on a seminar topic and get them to ask you questions afterwards.		
3 Play the game 'Speak for a minute' in your study group: try to speak for a minute on a topic pulled out of a hat.		
4 Choose a debate topic and split the study group into two teams, *For* and *Against*. After some preparation, debate the topic.		
5 Work together to make a list of functional phrases that are used for presenting and discussing different points of view.		
6 Make a recording of a television programme involving a lot of discussion, for example a political debate programme, and watch it together, stopping it occasionally to continue the debate among you.		

Now check the key for comments on this exercise.

Study groups for exams

You might want to prepare for your exams on your own, but you might be the kind of student who likes to sit with other people when they study and even talk about what you are revising. If so, it is important to discuss the kind of activities you will do in your group to prepare for your exams. In this way you will share the same expectations of exam preparation sessions. The discussion you have can be a good way to share and learn good study habits from other group members. You might decide to:

- sit together and revise quietly without talking (you might want to plan what time you will all take a collective break and how long it will be for)

- revise quietly on your own making notes and crib cards, and then come together to compare notes

- revise quietly, noting down important questions that you need answers to, and then come together and ask each other the questions you have written

- sit together and do a practice exam under exam conditions and compare your answers together afterwards.

Tip ✓ There are many different ways of preparing for exams, so do not be surprised if other students have different ideas from you. If your study group is not working for you, do not be afraid to leave it.

Remember

✔ Your study group is for *study*, not for fun, so the other members of your group do not have to be your friends.

✔ Think carefully before you let anyone join your study group because it might not be easy to ask them to leave if you later find they are not a suitable group member.

✔ If you want feedback from your study group on your work, make sure you tell them what aspects you want them to comment on.

✔ Try out your talk, seminar or presentation on your study group before you actually do it.

11 | Online group work

? Quiz
Self-evaluation

Read the statements and circle the answers that are true for you.

1	Online group work sounds easy. I can do it in bed!	agree | disagree | not sure
2	I wouldn't enjoy online group work because I don't like spending a lot of time on a computer.	agree | disagree | not sure
3	It's difficult to get to know people well when you don't meet them face to face, so it won't be a satisfying experience.	agree | disagree | not sure
4	Online group work is really convenient because you can work right up to the deadline and then submit the work at the last minute.	agree | disagree | not sure
5	The problem with working online all the time is that you can get distracted easily.	agree | disagree | not sure

Now check the key for comments on this exercise.

The nature of and reasons for online group work

Students doing online group work are usually studying at a distance from their university, although some campus courses may also use online group work elements in their courses. Online group work is used for exactly the same reasons as face-to-face group work: lecturers believe you will learn through cooperating, collaborating and negotiating with other students on a task.

There are many different ways of working online as a group, for example:

- using a virtual learning environment to meet and work together in real time (using a microphone and maybe video)

- using professional online-conferencing software to meet and work together in real time

- doing most of the work separately offline and then sharing the work on an online work space

- using email for most, or even all, of written communication

- making use of an online forum, message board or instant messaging programme

- communicating over the telephone and shared conference calls

Experiences of online group work can differ widely. It can sometimes be a very intense time: you might be given a tight deadline and need to work very hard. It might therefore be necessary to collaborate very closely with your group. For example, you might not be able to get on with your task until other students have finished theirs. It is also possible that the work will take up large amounts of your time.

In other situations, online group work may be less intense. You may find that after initial discussions, you spend most of your time working alone. You might only collaborate towards the end of the task when you need to put your work together and the actual group work may not be very time-consuming. Whatever your group work experience, it will provide you with learning opportunities and challenges.

The challenges of online group work

You might welcome the opportunity to do online group work and choose to do it as an option for one of your modules. On the other hand, you might have no choice about working in a group online. Whatever your situation, it will probably be new to you, and it is quite likely that you will have preconceptions about what it is like.

Having a *positive attitude* to online group work is the first step to being part of a successful online team. There are challenges to working like this, but you should understand that these challenges are something to learn from; overcoming the challenges is a large part of the task itself.

Group Work

Exercise 1

Read about the reasons why some students do not enjoy online group work.
Write 'Yes' if you agree with them or 'No' if you disagree. Make notes about
some strategies for overcoming the challenges.

Challenges of online group work	Yes / No	Strategies to overcome challenges
1 You do not get to know the other students properly because you never meet them.		
2 You might not always know what is happening as students could be online at irregular intervals.		
3 Some students might not have easy access to computers or the internet.		
4 Some students might not have the appropriate IT skills.		
5 It takes much longer to collaborate online than in face-to-face meetings, so it is not an efficient way to work.		
6 There are more likely to be misunderstandings when you communicate online.		
7 Others may take a long time to respond to a message, so it is difficult to move forward with an idea.		
8 If there are students in different parts of the world, it might be hard to find a convenient time for everyone to meet.		
9 You are more likely to have to solve problems on your own.		
10 It is hard to ensure that all group members work as a team, and some students might actively avoid work.		
11 It is more likely that there will be an imbalance of workload.		
12 Students are more likely to leave work to the last minute, leading to missed deadlines.		

Now check the key for answers and comments on this exercise.

Many students enjoy online group work, and their enthusiasm can bring its own benefits. If you are less convinced about the benefits of online group work, it is important to reflect on the benefits of this way of working.

Exercise 2

Read about the reasons why some students enjoy online group work. Write 'Yes' if you agree with them or 'No' if you disagree. Make notes about any additional comments.

Benefits of online group work	Yes / No	Additional comments
1 You can usually work at your own pace and at the time of day that suits you.		
2 If you are not very confident face to face, you might be more confident online and in an environment where you can *develop* your personal skills.		
3 You have more time to prepare what you want to communicate online, so you can have more thoughtful and meaningful interactions.		
4 You have a reason to improve your IT skills when you work online, and this has wider benefits, particularly in making use of specialized computer software.		
5 You improve your teamwork skills even more than you do when working face to face because you have to work harder to make your group function well.		
6 When working online with others, you can focus on the *content* of what they do or say rather than be distracted by superficial aspects such as appearance.		

Now check the key for answers and comments on this exercise.

Strategies for online group work

In earlier chapters we considered the importance of:

- getting to know each other

- building trust

- establishing ground rules

- assigning roles and responsibilities

- understanding the requirements of the task.

Online group work is no different. In fact, these elements are *even more important* in online group work because of the lack of face-to-face contact. The following ideas are examples of guidelines and activities that will give you a good chance of success in your online group work.

Get to know your online group members as well as you can and as quickly as you can

You will need to exploit the technology you have in order to get to know your team members. It can be harder to get to know people you do not meet regularly face to face, so you will need to make an effort to do this. Consider the time you spend getting to know your group members online as an *investment*. You will benefit later in the group work process from this investment of time.

Exercise 3

Read some suggestions below for getting to know your online team members. Which ones would work well? Can you see difficulties with any of them? Make notes about how these suggestions would work for you.

'Getting to know you' activities	Would it work well for you?
1 Write an introductory email about yourself and send it to your group members. Write individual responses to the emails that you get.	
2 Share photographs of each other.	

3 Become 'friends' on Facebook.	
4 Write a CV which includes your skills and background and share it with your group.	
5 Meet together online in a chat room and spend time asking and answering questions about each other (see *Getting to know you activities* in Chapter 2).	
6 Work together to create a group internet page showing your photographs, backgrounds, interests and skills.	
7 Complete a skills audit form (see Chapter 2, Exercise 3) and email it to your group members.	

Now the key for answers and comments on this exercise.

Build trust within your group

Building trust is essential to forming a successful online group. Trust grows when team members do things for each other, collaborate closely and meet agreed deadlines. If you can complete group activities in which these things happen, you will grow to trust each other. You can build trust in lots of ways, for example:

- **Writing each other's bio for your group internet page**

  This activity involves sharing your background and personal information with one of your group members, who then writes the bio for you. This gives the other member of the group control over an important aspect of your life, and can be a powerful way to build trust.

- **Setting up some meetings and being there on time**

  Arrange a series of meetings online. The frequency of the meetings will depend on how long your group work lasts: if you have a short time span, you might want a number of meetings on one day; if you have more time, you might want to have only one a day. Every time you appear at an arranged time, you will build more trust with your group.

Tips

✓ Arrange some meetings even if you do not have a lot of work to share. The purpose of the meetings is to build trust, not only to work.

✓ Arrange a way to communicate if you have IT problems (such as text, email, telephone) so your group members do not think you are unreliable.

admit
If you admit that something bad, unpleasant or embarrassing, you agree, often unwillingly, that it is true.

water-cooler chat
A water-cooler chat refers to the informal conversations that people have in their office or workplace around the water cooler.

- **Admitting to mistakes you make**

  Everybody makes mistakes sometimes, and sometimes it can be reassuring to see *other* people making mistakes. If you admit to mistakes, your team will appreciate your honesty and respect you. In return, they will be more open about difficulties they are having. Hiding mistakes is likely to cause more problems in the long run and generate distrust among the group.

- **Sharing and rotating responsibilities**

  Taking it in turns to do things is another good way to build trust. For example, after any meetings, you could take it in turns to write up the notes and send them out to the other group members, or take it in turn to write the agenda before the next meeting. When team members see other team members using power responsibly and passing it on, trust will usually grow and develop.

Build some social interaction into your group work

It is very important for you to spend time *socialising* with your online group as well as working. Although the reason for being in a group is to work, the work will be easier and more enjoyable if there is a social element to it. When colleagues in a professional environment have a meeting, there will usually be small talk before and after the formal discussion – you should behave in a similar way with your online group members. Here are some ways of benefiting from socialising with your group.

- **Have a real face-to-face meeting with your group if it is possible or convenient**

  If possible, meet your group face to face, even if it is only once. Do not feel you have to start working immediately you meet: there is plenty of time for that later. Spend the time to interact socially so that you start to *bond* as you get to know each other.

- **Write regular emails to your group**

  You should contact your group on a regular basis with regard to any group task. When you do so, make sure you start and finish the email with some comments about other things such as interests, hobbies, family, and the weather. These comments will make the work more fun, and over time you will get to know your team members well.

- **Have 'water cooler' chats with your team members**

  Use an instant messaging service online when you need a short break. When you are ready for a 'water cooler' break, open up your messaging service so others can see you are online. Then switch it off when you need to get back to work.

- **Have online coffee breaks together**

  Arrange a time for a break and a coffee, and meet online to chat and relax. Do not worry about work during the coffee break as that can come later.

Tips

- ✓ Be careful about making jokes or teasing group members online. It is harder to show you are making a joke online, so others might take you seriously and get upset.
- ✓ Be patient as the stages of group development that you progress through (as discussed in Chapter 4) are likely to take longer in online groups; group cohesion will come in time.

Tips

Remember

✓ Online group work can be challenging, but that challenge is part of the task.

✓ Keep in regular contact with your online group.

✓ Share other ways to communicate in case of technological difficulties.

✓ Spend time socialising and building trust with your group members.

12 | Learning from your experience of group work

Aims
- ✓ evaluate the group work experience
- ✓ set goals for the future
- ✓ learn from other students' experiences
- ✓ learn from lecturers' thoughts about group work

? Quiz
Self-evaluation

Read the statements and circle the answers that are true for you.

1	When I finish an assignment and I hand it in, that's it; I don't want to go back over it again.	agree | disagree | not sure
2	My lecturer should tell me what I need to learn.	agree | disagree | not sure
3	My course will cover all the skills and subject knowledge that I need to learn.	agree | disagree | not sure
4	Nobody is perfect: there will always be some things that I can't do very well.	agree | disagree | not sure
5	I don't want to spend all my time working! I need to relax after I have finished my work.	agree | disagree | not sure

Now check the key for comments on this exercise.

Evaluating the group work experience

You should always make the most of your experience of working in a particular group by thinking about it carefully and reflecting on your experiences. It is a good idea to consider how you performed, how your group performed and what you learned.

Even if you have done this already by doing a piece of reflective writing, you should continue to think about all aspects of your group work assignment. This will help you to carry on improving your skills and subject knowledge and gaining a good understanding of your strengths and weaknesses.

Exercise 1

Read the questions in the group evaluation form. Use them to help you to evaluate past group work performance and experience. Rather than answering 'Yes' or 'No', make notes on the *results* of what you did or did not do, and how you *feel* about your actions now. Use the opportunity to reflect on what you have done.

If you have not yet experienced significant group work activities, you can read about the experience of one of the students in Appendix 2 and try to answer the questions in the evaluation form based on their experience.

Group work evaluation form	
Evaluation of your group work performance	Comments
1 Did you start thinking about your assignment as soon as it was given to you?	
2 Did you spend some time thinking about the process of group work before you started on the actual assignment?	
3 Did you agree on ground rules at the start of your assignment?	
4 Did you allocate roles and responsibilities for your group members?	
5 Did you write a set of goals and objectives?	
6 Did you make a Gantt chart?	
7 Did you review your group's progress during the task?	
8 Did you review your performance during your group work?	
9 Did you review your group's performance during your group work?	
10 Did you give feedback to your group members about their work and performance during your group work?	
11 Did you meet your deadline comfortably?	
12 Were you happy with your mark for your group assignment?	
13 What skills did you improve during your group work?	
14 What subject knowledge did you improve during the presentation?	
15 What skills did you find that you need to improve?	
16 How could you improve the contribution you made to your group?	

Now check the key for comments on this exercise.

You should be able to identify the specific skills you need in order to participate successfully in group work in an English-speaking university context. This will help you to understand what you need to work on.

Exercise 2

Think about the skills that group work is meant to improve and write a skills audit review form. Think about your experience of group work and whether you were able to improve these skills or not. Make comments about any improvements you would like to make.

If you have not yet experienced significant group work activities, you can read about the experience of one of the students in Appendix 2 and complete a skills audit review form based on their experience.

Skills audit review			
	Improvement made (what?)	No change (why not?)	(More) improvements needed in this area
Presentation skills	*I definitely improved my presentation delivery skills. I gained confidence speaking in front of the class.*		*I want to improve my fluency even more so I don't have to think so much before I speak.*

Setting goals for the future

Glossary

fluency
Someone who can speak a language with fluency can speak it easily and correctly.

portal
On the Internet, a portal is a site that consists of links to other websites.

Now that you have identified the skills and subject knowledge you want to improve, you will need to think about *how* to make these improvements. Bear in mind that there will be considerations of time and resources, for example:

- the time period over which you would like to see the improvements that you have identified

- how much time you can allocate to making these improvements

- the resources you need to enable you to make these improvements

The skills and subject knowledge goals form on page 115 shows how a student might use a form to record their goals after their group work experience. Whether or not you have experienced group work, you may wish to think about the skills you wish to improve in order to perform well in group work. You can use this exercise to reflect on all the areas you have identified as needing improvement while you have been working through this book.

For example:

Skills and subject knowledge goals		
Skill area I want to improve	Time	Resources
I want to improve my English language fluency so that I can express myself better during group work and in presentations.	As soon as possible. I would like to see improvement over the next three months. I will allocate one evening a week and 20 minutes on other days to achieving this goal.	I will make use of the university English Club on Tuesday evenings. I will volunteer at the student union to improve my speaking skills.
Knowledge of Excel.	This is urgent. I will allocate one weekend this term for this.	I will work through the university online *Excel at Excel* module available through the university portal.

Learning from other students' experiences of group work

It can be useful and interesting to read about other students' experiences of group work, especially if you have not had a lot of experience of it yourself. In this way, you can:

- find out what to expect from group work

- understand that it is usual to have some difficulties during group work

- appreciate the value of group work.

There are six appendices following this chapter that will give you extra help in your group work. Appendix 2 has transcripts of two interviews with international students who talk about their experiences of group work. Reading about these experiences can help you to understand what to expect from group work in an English-speaking university. Exercises 3 and 4 in this chapter relate to this appendix. Appendix 3 has transcripts of two interviews with lecturers who use group work in their teaching. Reading these interviews will help you to understand why lecturers ask you to work in groups and what they expect from you. Exercises 5 and 6 in this chapter relate to this appendix.

Exercise 3

Read about a student's experience of group work in Appendix 2 and make notes to answer the questions.

Qavitha's experience of group work	
1 Find an example of Qavitha being a proactive team member and doing something to help her team.	
2 Find an example of Qavitha being aware of one of her own weaknesses?	
3 What did Qavitha do to overcome her weakness?	
4 What difficulties did Qavitha face when she first came to her university?	
5 What helped her to overcome these difficulties?	
6 Qavitha uses the example of an apple to explain the benefits of group work. What point is she making?	
7 You can work in groups outside the group work given by your lecturers. What example of this does Qavitha give?	
8 What important quality did Qavitha learn from working in groups?	
9 Do you think the argument in Qavitha's group was damaging to the group, or was it beneficial?	
10 Do you think Qavitha learned anything from her group work experience in Malaysia?	

Now check the key for answers and comments on this exercise.

Exercise 4

Read about another student's experience of group work in Appendix 2 and make notes to answer the questions.

Chen's experience of group work	
1 Identify the important thing Chen did which showed her being proactive and courageous.	
2 Chen and her friend volunteered to do the introduction for a whole group presentation. What effect do you think this had on the group?	
3 Can you find an example of group members reaching a compromise in Chen's description of her group work?	
4 How did Chen and her group try to solve the problem of the student who was always late?	
5 Do you think there is anything else that Chen and her group could have done to try to solve the problem of the student being late?	
6 What does Chen think are the most important things you can learn during group work?	
7 According to Chen, international students need courage. What does she think they need it for?	
8 Chen says that working with people from different countries is useful. What reasons does she give?	

Now check the key for answers and comments on this exercise.

Learning from lecturers' experiences of group work

It can be also be very beneficial to read what university lecturers say about group work. By doing this you can:

- understand why they give you group work to do

- understand what they expect from you during group work

- get advice on how to behave during group work.

Exercise 5

Read an interview with a lecturer in Appendix 3 and make notes to answer to the questions.

Helen's experiences of group work as a lecturer	
1 It is important to get to know your group members as soon as you can. What does Helen do to make sure her group members get to know each other in her class?	
2 Why does Helen think it is important for her students to write a list of ground rules and to sign it?	
3 What is the key to a successful group presentation, according to Helen?	
4 What skills does Helen think students can improve during group work?	
5 Helen makes an important link between working in an international group and developing critical thinking skills. What is it?	
6 Do you like Helen's system of giving students two marks (an individual mark and a group mark)? Why/Why not?	
7 Helen thinks groups generally score higher than individuals in coursework. What does this show?	
8 Does Helen penalize students who come to her with group problems?	

Now check the key for answers and comments on this exercise.

Exercise 6

Read the interview with Pat, another lecturer, in Appendix 3 and make notes to answer the questions.

Pat's experiences of group work as a lecturer	
1 Why does Pat get his trainee teachers to teach their early classes together as a group?	
2 Pat comments on two common problems that often crop up in group work. What are they?	
3 Do you think Pat minds if students come to ask him for help?	
4 What particular qualities does Pat focus on when he talks about what students learn from group work?	
5 Why should you not worry too much when things go wrong during group work?	
6 What does Pat think you should do if you have group problems?	

Now check the key for answers and comments on this exercise.

Remember

✔ Always reflect on your group work experience so you learn as much as you can from it.

✔ Think about your weaknesses and what you can do to overcome them.

✔ Listen and read about other people's experiences so you can learn from them.

✔ Always be willing to learn from life experiences so you can change and adapt to achieve what you want.

Appendix 1 – Useful phrases

Useful phrases that you have been introduced to throughout the book are reproduced here in Appendix 1 for easy reference. Other useful phrases have been added to provide an even more comprehensive list for use during group work.

Getting a meeting started

- Is everybody here yet?
- Has anybody seen (Juan)?
- Is it time to start yet?
- Have we got enough (chairs)?
- Has everyone brought (their notes on the topic)?
- Can someone organize (the coffee)?
- Do we all know where the bathrooms are?
- Shall we start, then?
- Are we ready to start?

Introducing a group member

- Can I introduce (Michelle)?
- She's been in (Scotland) for (six months) now.
- She's just come over from (France).
- She's living (in the halls of residence in a flat with other students).
- She told me she likes (keeping fit) and she's quite keen on (swimming).
- She doesn't think her English is very good, but I can understand her!

Negotiating roles

- Who would like to (chair the meeting)?
- I think (David) should be (group secretary) because he's (got clear handwriting).
- What about (Faiz) for the role of (IT supervisor)?
- I'd really like to take on the role of (designer).
- I think I'd be good in the role of (social organizer) because I'm good at (communicating).
- My experience in (my uncle's business) means that I would make a good (group accountant).
- I know you want that role, but would you consider me for it?
- I don't think I'd be suitable for that. I'm not very good at (complex calculations).
- I'm sorry, but I'm not keen on being (the architect). How about if I do (the planning)?

Negotiating what to do during group work

- I think we should (finish collecting the data now).
- I think we should consider (doing it freehand).

- How about we (stop and start again in the morning)?
- How about (building a model first)?
- What about if we (did it in Excel)?
- I wonder if we could (get some help from the document production centre)?
- Why don't we (get the readings this afternoon)?
- What do the rest of you think?
- Why do you want to do that?
- Do you think it would be useful to talk about (the next meeting)?
- I'm not sure whether discussing (the last report) would be useful.
- I'm not sure how (this information) is useful.
- Can we agree on that?
- We've got to decide (which one to choose).

Giving your opinion, agreeing and disagreeing

- Yes, absolutely!
- That's true. I hadn't thought of it like that.
- Well, I agree up to a point.
- The way I see it is like this.
- Can I just make a point here?
- I think you have a point, but don't forget (the deadline is 4.00 p.m. tomorrow!)
- I know what you're saying, but I think we should (finish the artwork first).
- Maybe, but I still believe we're in danger of (running out of time).
- I'm sorry, I know that's your opinion, but I can't agree.
- Have you tried looking at it from the point of view of (cost)?

Giving feedback to your peers

- Michelle's got a good point.
- Great. I think that's excellent.
- I like this part when you (discuss the materials), but I think this part here could be improved.
- Can I make some suggestions about (the introduction)? Why don't you say more about (our aims)?
- Don't you think it would be better to focus a bit more on (the discussion) rather than (the methodology)?
- I thought we had decided you would cover (the results from the river), not (the seabed)?
- I like what you've written, but I think it would be even better if you added/changed/moved (this part).

Showing you are listening properly to your other group members

- Mmm.
- Right.
- I see.
- Go on. I'm listening.
- I think I can imagine how you feel.

- How do you feel about that?
- Do you want to say more about that?

Checking information

- I see. So you're saying (you want me to redo it).
- I'm not sure what you mean by (changing the introduction).
- Could you go over that again?
- What was it you meant by (rephrasing the second paragraph)?
- I'm not sure I follow.

Showing your thoughts in reflective writing

- I think one of the most challenging aspects of the assignment was (working online).
- One of the hardest things to deal with was (not knowing what was going to happen next).
- It was difficult to deal with (the data in the spreadsheets).
- If I did a similar assignment again I would (make sure I had everything I needed before I started).
- I hadn't expected (the weather to make things so hard).
- I didn't expect to (have problems with the technology).
- I/We tried to deal with the problem by (talking it through).
- With hindsight, it would have been a good idea to (plan more thoroughly).
- At least it has helped me to improve my (teamwork skills).
- I found I was able to (communicate quite effectively), but I realize I need to work on (my presentation skills).
- I learned that (building relationships) is more important than (getting results).

Referring to group members during a presentation

- As (Mohammed) said earlier, we (started our project in February).
- (Michelle) will say a bit more about (this aspect of our work) later on.
- I'll be focusing on (the fieldwork), (Grant) will talk about (analysing the data) and (Sylvia) will be discussing (our results).
- Now I'll hand over to (Martine), who will (conclude our presentation).
- Thanks for the question; I'll try to answer it as best I can.
- That's a great question, but I think (Susan) could answer it best.
- wI'd like to bring in (Bing) to answer that question.

Appendix 2 – Interviews with students about group work

Chapter 12, pages 116–117

Reading the following interviews with two students will help you to understand the benefits and challenges of group work.

Qavitha's experience

Qavitha comes from Malaysia and is studying for a BSc in Psychology in an English-speaking university. Here she answers some questions about her experiences of group work.

How many students were in your group and who were they?

1 Five. We were a mix of British and international students.

What was the task?

2 It was a qualitative piece of research work. We had to combine all our ideas to make up a questionnaire for how students experience shopping. So we had to combine ideas and make up a questionnaire and then present it to one of our colleagues.

How long did the assignment last?

3 It took place over a month. But that was broken down into shorter periods. So each week we had to add another bit and then another bit. And then at the end we had to submit the whole thing.

How often did you meet up with your team members?

4 When we were doing the questionnaire, we met for two hours every day for three days – it was quite a busy time.

How did you organize your meetings?

5 Usually by email ... or when we saw each other in class, we just talked to each other and organized them. Sometimes we booked a room in the library for our group meeting. I was in charge of booking the room and emailing out to my friends and telling them the time – and I would get the key.

Group Work

How did you get the responsibility for booking the room for your meetings?

6

> I volunteered for that role[1]. There was another student who lived a long way from the university and it wasn't easy for her to do that sort of thing ... I just volunteered for it.

Did you have any weak members of the group?

7

> Yes, that would be me! I was quite confused about what to do. I struggled with qualitative research questions. In Malaysia, I had worked with quantitative questions and likeart scales. But when it came to qualitative research it was so new to me. I didn't really understand the meaning of open-ended questions. I was the weak one and they tried to explain to me a few times. I went to my personal tutor[2] and asked her to help me with it. She could help me out and explain and tell me what I needed to do. She said if you need to come back again, you can. So I approached group members and my tutor for help.

Did your group members help you?

8

> Yes, they helped me. The group helped me a lot. Knowing that I'm an international student and English is my second language, they really helped me.

Is it harder for you having English as a second language?

9

> Well, when I first came here I couldn't speak properly. I didn't answer questions properly. If somebody asked me something, I would beat around the bush and then come back to the proper answer. And I couldn't understand the accent. And saying things like 'cheers'. And using cutlery was a big thing for me. Then my friends helped[3] me saying, 'You shouldn't use this word here. Use this word here.' It really helped me.

Why do you think your teachers give you group work?

10

> I think in individual work you are just giving your own ideas. In group work you collaborate and you develop more. You put lots of ideas into the work. Imagine if you describe an apple, some people might say 'it's round', some people might say 'it's green' – you will get lots of different ideas from group work, whereas if you do individual work, you just get one idea. The different ideas you get makes group work much better than individual work. You learn more.

So you think you learn more in a group?

11

> Yes. If I am preparing for an exam, I would rather be in a group[4] than sitting down alone at home. After ten minutes I would be bored!

Do you think you learn more about your subject working in a group?

12

> Yes. And if I need help from people, they are there to help in group work[5]. But if I'm alone, I don't have anyone to communicate with. Having more ideas is good. Two heads are better than one.

What else do you learn from group work?

13

> Being patient! Being very, very patient. You never know what somebody is really thinking. When someone says something you don't like, you shouldn't just immediately say 'You're wrong.'[6] You should have the patience to listen and understand what they mean and then say 'fine' and try to evaluate it. Then think how you can use the idea in the group assignment. Because sometimes somebody might suggest something which you can't use in the assignment, but you have to say why. You have to say 'this can't be used because …' And even if it's not right, you can try to change it a bit to fit it in.

Were there some difficulties in working as a group?

14

> Yes. There was an argument. One of us didn't agree with somebody else. But at the end of the day we came up with a solution. We said, 'Fine. Instead of fighting this is how it's going to be. This is what we're going to do.' And everybody agreed to it. We each contributed our ideas and we just did it.

How did the argument happen?

15

> We had to write quite a few questions. Everyone was giving out ideas. There was quite a commotion. There was a fight! But we managed to get over it after ten or fifteen minutes. We realized that two hours together would be a long time if we were fighting. Instead we decided that everyone would give an idea, you give an idea, you give an idea, you give an idea, and that's how we managed it.

Group Work

So you decided to include everyone's idea?

16

> Yes, exactly. We said to the first person, 'OK what do you want to focus on?' and, 'OK, you do that'. And we went round to each person, who said what they wanted to do.
>
> Each five of us had a different idea and that made it easier in the end. Earlier we were arguing, saying, 'No we shouldn't do this, we shouldn't do that', everybody was trying to give a solution and nobody knew what to do and that's when the fight started[7]. That's when somebody just said, 'OK, let's all say what we each want to do and we'll put it together.'

Had you done group work in Malaysia before coming to the UK?

17

> Yes. It was a distressing time for me. I was given the job of preparing the slides. But everyone had different ideas, so I didn't know what to put on the slides. They gave me all their different ideas and told me to put them all in the slides. When they saw my slides, they all said I had made a terrible mistake and that they didn't trust me. Everyone said, 'This is not what we asked you to do'. And I just tried to put everything in. They told me to leave it. They said, 'Just do the talking. We'll give you cue cards'. I thought, 'OK fine'. Later that day one of the group members asked me what idea I had contributed to the presentation. I explained that because I had been doing the slides, I hadn't prepared my own content. He told me I was very irresponsible. So I did prepare something and I sent it to him and he said it was rubbish. He said that he would prepare everything and that I just had to read the cue card during the presentation. On the day of the presentation nobody knew what was going on. He took complete control[8]. I didn't know which part of the presentation I was giving. He just told me that he would pull me in when I needed to talk. But he didn't even do that. He just expected me to look at the slide and to know when to talk. At the end he told me that I had screwed up his whole assignment.

Comment and analysis of Qavitha's experience

The comment and analysis below provides insights on the interview with Qavitha. Each note relates to a numbered part of the interview.

Note 1

Notice how Qavitha supported her group by volunteering for a responsibility. She was proactive and showed good teamworking skills.

Note 2

Qavitha found the work difficult but she didn't struggle on her own. She went to her personal tutor for help who was happy to support her.

Note 3

Home students can be a great source of support for international students. As an international student you should do what you can to meet home students as much as possible. They will also benefit from your experience, skills and the different outlook that you bring to things.

Note 4

Lecturers will organize group work for you, but they will not organize things like group revision sessions. Think about organizing a study group so you can gain the benefits of group work outside formal group assignments.

Note 5

Qavitha really shows how group work can provide support because the group are always there to help you and you will always have more ideas if you work in a group.

Note 6

Qavitha shows a good understanding of the need to treat group members with respect. You need to listen carefully to everybody's ideas and try to include them in your group work if you can, even if you need to change them a bit.

Note 7

Qavitha's group argued because they got frustrated at their lack of progress. They all had different ideas about what to do and they couldn't move forward. They solved their problem by discussion and agreeing to include everyone's ideas.

Note 8

Qavitha was unlucky to be in a group with someone who demanded complete control over the group work. This can be a difficult situation to deal with. Her group allowed the dominant student to take control. Strong students can dominate individual students but it is harder for them to dominate a whole group if the group works together.

Group Work

Chen's experience

Chen comes from mainland China. She is doing a postgraduate degree in an English-speaking university after finishing her BSc in Tourism at the same university.

What was the task?

1

> We had to give a group presentation for our Tourism course. The task for our group was to identify the importance of heritage in tourism. We had to do an assignment and give a group presentation on the topic.

How long were you given for the assignment?

2

> Three or four weeks, but we didn't start it early.

Could you choose your group members yourselves?

3

> Yes, we could choose the group members ourselves.

How did you choose your group members?

4

> I'm not quite sure. At that time there were not many Chinese students in our class. Most students were English. There were some students from the Caribbean. In fact, it was difficult for us to find group members. We don't know if the other students want us to join with them. It's so hard![1] I don't know why! Before we had done some group work and I just went up to the Caribbean girl and asked her. She seemed quite nice and I asked her if she had a group already and I asked her if me and my friend could join her in a group and she said OK. So this time we naturally formed a group. And her friend was friends with an English boy, so she asked him to join, so we had a group of five, with one English boy, two Caribbean girls and two Chinese girls. A very international group!

How did you divide up the work that needed to be done?

5

> Actually, this task was quite simple. We came up with different ideas because we are from three different countries. So me and my Chinese friend came up with heritage ideas in China, the Caribbean girls came up with ideas from the Caribbean and the English boy came up with ideas about heritage in British tourism[2]. We thought it would be diverse and good. We thought it was quite easy.

Did you have different responsibilities for different things?

6

> Not really. You had to finish your own PowerPoint. Then we sent all these to one person who put them together, and then sent this whole thing to each group member so we could see what it was going to be like.

But how did you organize who did the introduction and the conclusion for the whole presentation?

7

> We asked for volunteers. Me and my Chinese friend volunteered to do the introduction for the whole presentation[3], and the English boy volunteered to do the conclusion. But then each part we had we did our own introductions again. In our part we decided to do four aspects of heritage in China and so we did two each.

Did you have any disagreements?

8

> Not that serious, but we did have some with the PowerPoint[4]. We had different ideas about making a good PowerPoint. Me and my Chinese friend thought their words were too simple. And they thought we had written too many words. But that is our way of doing PowerPoint. We think that if you just put one sentence that may be too easy. Finally it was OK, we just all changed it a little bit.

Did you have a weak member of the group?

9

> One of the girls was a little bit lazy. We had several group meetings. She was always really late. The most serious thing was the final day when we had to submit our work. We had to meet the deadline but she was really late. We had to wait for her a long time. She forgot lots of things, like the memory stick. She had left it at home. So when she finally came back, it was a really busy time and it was difficult to get to the printer because it was being used by others. We had been waiting there for a long time. In the end we sorted it out. Her friend said she is always like that.

Did you say anything to her to try to improve her contribution to the group?

10

> Yes, we did. For the group meetings we asked her to come earlier to the meetings. She said OK but then she was always still late after that[5]. The most annoying thing was to be very late on the day that you are going to submit the assignment.

Group Work

So there wasn't really a solution to her being late?

11
> Not really, no. You can't really do anything because you are in a group. You can't just say 'You're not good'. One of the group members who knew her quite well got angry with her and shouted a bit.

Why do you think your teacher asked you to do your work in a group rather than separately?

12
> Well, individual work is just your own ideas but group work is more – well, you have to communicate and coordinate. If you only have your own idea, it might be really limited. I have found through doing group work that the way we think is totally different from the way that local students think. But it's interesting. It's useful … because you hear ideas that you had never thought of before. It inspires you to think in a totally different way from the way you usually think.

Can you give an example of that?

13
> Well, when we were brainstorming for different ideas, me and my Chinese friend came up with similar ideas. But the English boy came up with a new idea. Something we had never thought of before. But it still makes sense. It could still be good work. Just really different.

What other things did you learn from working in a group?

14
> We had to learn how to communicate[6], to tell group members how we were not very happy with them being late. Also, sometimes we were working hard but one of the group members was watching football on his laptop. We had to say, 'What do you think you are doing? We are working hard here.' At first, we were a little bit afraid to say what we thought. But then finally we did tell the other group members that they had to work harder.

How did your group presentation go?

15

> It was quite good. Actually the English boy asked us to dress in our traditional costumes. He was wearing a suit but we didn't have our traditional costumes from our own countries. We didn't want to. So on that day he wore a suit, but we just wore our own clothes. Me and my Chinese friend made a very good job of the first few PowerPoint slides and the Caribbean girls can talk very well and also the English boy. It worked well[7].

What advice would you give to international students doing group work?

16

> I know a lot of Chinese students have a lot of other Chinese students in their class, so sometimes they only get together with other Chinese students. My advice is that you have to have courage and confidence. Because most of the time they are just afraid to talk and think that others are thinking that they are not good enough to be their group members. But you have to ask! You have to at least try. And it's quite good because if you can get in a mixed nationality group, you can get a lot of ideas[8].

> It's only after I had done the group work that I realized that our way of thinking is quite different. So you learn a lot. That is the point of why you are studying here.

Comment and analysis of Chen's experience

The comment and analysis below provides insights on the interview with Chen. Each note relates to a numbered part of the interview.

Note 1

It seems it can be very difficult for some international students to approach home students and students from other countries about forming a group. It is a good idea to try to make contact with other students from different countries early on in your course. Then you can build on the relationships as your course progresses.

Note 2

Chen discusses the value of having a diverse group. Because Chen had students from different parts of the world in her group, it was easy to get a wide variety of input into the group work. The diversity of the group made the group work much easier than if they had all had the same background.

Note 3

Chen and her group members volunteered to take on responsibility for parts of the group task. This demonstrates a good commitment to teamwork and helped strengthen the group.

Note 4

Chen's description of the digital presentation issue is a very good example of different students wanting different things. Chen and her Chinese friend wanted a lot of words on the slides, whereas her other group members wanted short simple sentences on the slides. In the end the students compromised and they both changed their work a little to find a middle way.

Note 5

Although Chen and her friends tried to talk to the group member who was always late, she didn't change her behaviour. Even if this happens to you, you should continue to try to work with the difficult group member right up until the end of the task. Then you can gain the benefit of the difficult experience you have had.

Note 6

Chen believes that through doing group work she learned how to communicate more effectively and let others in the group know how she felt about them.

Note 7

This comment shows again that Chen learned, from group work, that there are many different ways of doing things successfully.

Note 8

Chen's final remarks summarize the value of working with others: you learn how different people think and this means you learn a lot. In English-speaking universities this learning is considered to be very important.

Appendix 3 – Interviews with lecturers about group work

Chapter 12, pages 118–119

The following interviews with two lecturers will help you to understand what they think about group work and why they give it to students.

Helen's view

Helen is a lecturer in English for Academic Purposes (EAP) in an English-speaking university.

What group work assignments do you give your students?

1   I give my students group presentations. So they have to work together to research and deliver the presentation.

What do they have to present?

2   They have to choose an everyday product that they use and research it from a social, economic or sustainable point of view: for example, the working conditions that the workers who produce the product work in. So the students practise their research skills and their critical-thinking skills.

How do you assess the students?

3   I give them an individual mark, which reflects their individual contribution, and a group mark.

How long do you give them for their assignment?

4   Research shows that students need a lot of time for group work. I give them a long time. I give them the assignment brief early on in the term. Altogether they had six or seven weeks to do the assignment.

How do you prepare your students for group work?

5   I think it's really important that students understand what group work means before they start on the task[1]. I actually ask them to work in pairs first of all to give a mini-presentation about group work to the class. This is to prepare them for working in groups and to help them to get to know each other.

Group Work

Can the students choose their own group members?

6
> Yes, the groups are self-selecting.

Are there ever difficulties with forming groups?

7
> Sometimes there are. This year, with one class, they found it difficult to make their groups, but the other class did it really easily.

What do you do to support the students in their group work?

8
> I give them a group tutorial. They have to come with their set of ground rules that they have written and signed and their topic for their presentation.

So you ask them to write their own ground rules?

9
> Yes, I think it's important for them to do that[2], to understand their responsibilities and to consciously understand what they are agreeing to do.

Do your students have to do some reflection on their group work?

10
> Yes. They have to write a reflective piece based on their group work and presentation. They need to think about the whole assignment and they have a video recording of their presentation to help them.

What do you think students learn from doing a group work presentation as opposed to an individual presentation?

11
> They have to learn to manage their time. They have to physically meet up in order to succeed. The students who don't do that – who just prepare it individually and then meet up on the day and put it together – those are the least successful presentations[3] because there is no coherence. So there has to be cooperation between the group members.

What other things do students learn from group work?

12

The aim is to increase students' cooperation, their team skills, their allocation of responsibilities and to become aware of their strengths and weaknesses.

Does group work improve students' subject knowledge as well as teamwork skills?

13

When students work in mixed nationality groups, they get new perspectives on the topic that they couldn't possibly get as an individual[4]. For example, one group did a presentation on batteries, and one of the Chinese students had personal experience of the health risks of working in battery factories that the other students were completely unaware of. The international perspective they can bring to the task deepens their engagement with the issues around the products.

So students get new ideas from the other students?

14

The opening up of multiple perspectives on issues is crucial to developing students' critical-thinking skills[5]. Once you understand that something can be viewed from different perspectives – that is critical thinking. It's hard to see other perspectives when you are working on your own.

Do you think it is fair to give everyone in the group the same mark?

15

It might not be. In my assignments I give a group mark and an individual mark and students like that. I know that students sometimes think it's not fair that they all get the same mark but some students worked harder than others.

Do students get better marks when they work in groups?

16

I think so. Usually group work marks are higher than individual marks because students perform better as a group. The good students pull up the weaker students rather than the weak students pulling down the top students.

What difficulties do groups have?

17

It's difficult to know because students often don't come to us when they have problems. We sometimes don't know if some of the students aren't pulling their weight. I think there can be cultural issues between group members.

Group Work

What advice do you give to groups about dealing with problems?

18 I think the students need guidelines so they know what to do if their group is having problems. They should follow the guidelines to resolve their issues. The guidelines will include information about how and when to approach the tutor if they need to.

So the students wouldn't be penalised if they come to their tutor for help?

19 No. They should try to address the issues themselves first and then they can come to their tutor if they need to.

Comment and analysis of Helen's experience

The comment and analysis below provides insights on the interview with Helen. Each note relates to a numbered part of the interview.

Note 1

Helen wants her students to think about the process of group work before they actually start on their group task. You may have a teacher who helps you to do this or you may have to do it yourself. If you are well prepared for your group work, you are likely to make a better job of it and get a higher mark.

Note 2

You may have a teacher who asks you to write ground rules for your group. You may even be given ground rules. Alternatively, your teacher might not address this issue. In this case it will be up to you and the other students in your group to agree to use ground rules. It is highly likely that your group will function more effectively with ground rules to guide your behaviour and to make you aware of your responsibilities towards the group.

Note 3

Notice what Helen thinks makes a poor group presentation: when students work separately on the individual parts of the presentation and then put them together quickly before delivering it. It is important to make a group presentation which goes together well, not a series of individual presentations.

Note 4

Helen believes that learning in mixed nationality groups can greatly enhance student learning. It may feel more difficult to work in a mixed nationality group at first, but the benefits to your learning in the long run can be considerable.

Note 5

Helen thinks that group work improves students' critical-thinking skills.

Group Work

Pat's view

Pat teaches on a teacher-training course in an English-language speaking university.

What sort of group work assignments do you set your students?

1
> My students are learning to be teachers. I put them in groups and they have to team teach. That means teaching a class together. They have to plan the lesson, prepare the materials, write a lesson plan, and then teach the class.

How long do they have for their assignment?

2
> They get their assignment brief a long time in advance[1], so they can start to think about it ahead of time. But they don't know the details of the class until a few days beforehand. From start to finish the assignment period may be about six or eight weeks.

How many students were in the group?

3
> Three students.

Can students choose their own groups?

4
> Usually, yes. But sometimes I will ask some students to work together or to work apart if I think they will benefit from the experience.

Why do you get the students to do it in groups rather than individually?

5
> The results are better![2] The students are just learning to be teachers. They need to build up their knowledge and their confidence. They can support each other in the classroom. They can pool their ideas and take the best ones. The lessons that the groups give are far better than individually taught classes at this level.

How do you assess the students?

6
> They get one group mark for their group assignment.

Do the students think it's fair that they all get the same mark?

7

I think so. I give them a lot of feedback with their mark. They understand that they need to work together to give a good lesson. It needs to hang together well. If they just do their bits independently of each other, then it isn't a good lesson. To me it makes sense to give them all the same mark.

What difficulties do groups face?

8

Well, there are personality clashes sometimes. When you get two really strong personalities in one group, you can have power struggles. And you can get students with different levels of motivation. It can be hard when you see a student who is really motivated having to deal with a student who isn't so motivated[3].

How do you support students in their group work?

9

I give them group tutorials. I talk to them and try to find out how things are going. They can email me whenever they need to.

Can students come to you for help if they are having problems?

10

Of course. When they ask for too much help, I will just say something like, 'Well, I think you need to sort that out for yourselves.' It's very rare that I actually need to intervene in the group work.

Do you give your students ground rules for their group work?

11

No, I don't. I know that some teachers do this[4]. I leave it to the students to work it out. I don't want to interfere in their group work too much.

What other things do students learn from group work?

12

I think one of the most important things that students can learn is the value and importance of *having* good colleagues and *being* a good colleague. This is especially important for my students, who will need to build strong relationships with their colleagues when they are working as teachers. They need to understand the value of being able to ask for and to offer help.

Group Work

What other things do students learn from group work?

13

> I think they learn things when things go wrong. I think students are a bit more ambitious and brave in a group, which means sometimes things don't go well[5]. But you can learn a lot from making mistakes.

Do you ask your students to reflect on their group work?

14

> Yes. This is really important! What is the point of doing something if you don't learn from the experience? Reflection is when you show what you have learned from your experience, how you will do it better next time.

What advice would you give to students who have problems with their group work?

15

> My advice would be to face up to the problem early on. For example, if there is a group member who is missing meetings and not contributing, then this problem is only going to get worse. Students need to be brave and to call a meeting and to talk about things when they are not going well[6].

Comment and analysis of Pat's experience

The comment and analysis below provides insights on the interview with Pat. Each note relates to a numbered part of the interview.

Note 1

Both Pat and Helen give students their groups assignments well in advance. You should use the time you are given to start thinking about your assignment early on.

Note 2

Pat thinks that in certain situations groups can outperform individuals. He expects his students to support each other and learn from each other.

Note 3

Your lecturers understand that group work can be very challenging at times. That is one reason why they give it to you. They think that having to deal with unmotivated group members is a good opportunity for students to learn teamwork skills.

Note 4

Pat and Helen's different approaches to ground rules show there are differences in the ways lecturers do things. You need to read your assignment brief carefully to make sure you are following the guidelines. For example, if you are asked to draw up group ground rules but fail to do so, you are likely to lose marks.

Note 5

The product of your group work doesn't always have to be a great success. The value of learning from group work lies in the experience. If you produce something that is not very good but shows that you have learned a lot, you can still get a good mark. The teachers are interested in the process you went through and what skills you developed more than the product you ended up with.

Note 6

Helen and Pat's comments show that they, like other teachers in English-speaking universities, believe that group work is an important learning tool for their students. They want their students to understand the value of group work, engage in group work, and then reflect on their experience to show what they have learned.

Appendix 4 – Skills, abilities and qualities for group work

The following is a complete list of skills, abilities and qualities that facilitate group work and encourage participants to work effectively in groups. It is not expected that all students will possess such qualities and abilities, but they are ones that you should try to work towards.

It is important that you try to apply these skills, abilities and qualities to yourself rather than use them to criticize others. You will notice that many of them such as being patient, tactful, tolerant and sensitive to other's feelings are qualities that help deal with other group members who might lack certain qualities.

Students working in groups need to do the following:

- Listen to others
- Communicate well
- Make suggestions
- Put forward and defend a point of view
- Cooperate with others
- Question ideas and opinions
- Persuade others
- Encourage others
- Collaborate with others
- Participate in discussions and activities
- Share ideas and opinions
- Empathize with others
- Be patient
- Be thoughtful
- Be tolerant
- Be trustworthy
- Be fair
- Be tactful
- Be sensitive to other's feelings
- Be flexible
- Be prepared to compromise
- Be willing to negotiate
- Be open-minded
- Be honest with each other

- Be positive
- Be constructive
- Be committed
- Give and receive feedback constructively
- Respect others
- Recognize the strengths of others
- Rely on others and be reliable
- Be helpful and supportive of the group
- Be motivated and motivate others
- Make collective decisions
- Show understanding
- Lead and delegate
- Follow instructions
- Allocate responsibilities
- Be innovative
- Solve problems
- Reflect
- Use initiative
- Think critically
- Brainstorm
- Be creative
- Take responsibility
- Be disciplined
- Work hard

Appendix 5 – Useful forms and activities

Chapter 2, page 18

Nice to meet you!

Work in pairs. Take it in turns to ask each other the following questions. Make notes of the answers.

1 Full name: ———————————————————————

2 Name to be used in the group/Nickname: ————————————

3 Nationality: ————————————————————————

4 First language: —————————————————————————

5 Languages you can speak: ———————————————————

6 Currently living: ————————————————————————

7 Course: ————————————————————————————

8 Reasons for choosing this course: ————————————————

———————————————————————————————

9 Hobbies: ————————————————————————————

———————————————————————————————

10 Plans following this course: ——————————————————

———————————————————————————————

———————————————————————————————

When you have finished come together as a group and introduce your partner to the rest of the group. Partners should give more information, correct the information being given, and ask and answer more questions. This will generate a rewarding 'getting to know each other' session.

Chapter 2, page 19

Skills audit			
	Need to improve skills	Skills adequate	Skills good
1 *Written communication skills in English*: able to write fluently in English without making serious grammar mistakes			
2 *Spoken communication skills in English*: able to discuss things in English, give points of view, and justify opinions			
3 *Pronunciation skills*: having good enough pronunciation so that people can easily understand you when you speak			
4 *Presentation skills*: able to give an adequate formal presentation in English in front of others			
5 *IT skills*: able to carry out a range of practical tasks using a variety of computer programmes such as word processing, designing slides for presentations and making posters			
6 *Numeracy skills*: good with numbers when carrying out tasks such as costing, budgeting and keeping accounts			
7 *Teamwork skills*: able to work together with other students, negotiate compromise and share ideas			
8 *Reading and note-taking skills*: able to read long texts quickly and easily, understand them and take useful notes that can be understood later			

Chapter 2, page 20

Sharing experiences

1 Think about something you learned to do recently, e.g. driving or speaking another language.

  a Was it a good learning experience, or not?

  b What made it a good or a bad learning experience?

  _____

  _____

2 Think about a really good teacher that you had when you were at school.

  a What made this teacher special?

  b How did this affect the way you worked?

  _____

  _____

3 Think about a subject that you did not like at school.

  a What made you dislike the subject?

  b Could anything have been done to make it better?

  _____

  _____

4 Have you ever worked in a group before? If so:

  a What made it a good experience?

  b What did you learn from it?

  _____

  _____

5 Think about something you have done that needed courage and took you out of your comfort zone, e.g., doing something for the first time, or doing something you did not like or did not want to do.

  a How did you face your fear of doing it?

  b What did you learn from it?

  _____

  _____

Chapter 2, page 20

Group skills overview		
Group member's name	Has particular skills in ...	Has experience of ...

Chapter 2, page 26

Group contact form					
Name	Email address	Mobile number	Landline number	When not to call	Best way to get in touch

Chapter 5, page 56

My contribution to the team			
My learning style according to the Watchers/Doers, Thinkers/Feelers model	My personality type according to I or E, S or N, T or F, J or P	The role that I am likely to adopt in my group	What I will contribute to the team

Chapter 6, page 61

Self-evaluation form

	Never ⟶ Always				
1 I attend group meetings.	1	2	3	4	5
2 I am well prepared for group meetings.	1	2	3	4	5
3 I listen to my group members and show respect for what they are saying.	1	2	3	4	5
4 I contribute to meetings by giving my ideas.	1	2	3	4	5
5 I offer help to my group members when they need it.	1	2	3	4	5
6 I complete the tasks I have been assigned or I am on track with the tasks I have been assigned.	1	2	3	4	5
7 I am open-minded and make compromises where necessary.	1	2	3	4	5
8 I am approachable when my team members need to contact me and ask me something.	1	2	3	4	5

I have reflected on my performance and I could improve it by:

1 _____

2 _____

3 _____

4 _____

Chapter 6, page 63

Group evaluation form	Yes	Don't know	Don't think so
1 We have regular group meetings.			
2 We know what we are going to do when we meet as a group.			
3 Group members are keen to help each other when help is needed.			
4 Group members feel comfortable asking for help.			
5 When we have group discussions, group members feel comfortable giving their opinions.			
6 Everybody contributes when there is a group discussion.			
7 Group members are well suited to their group roles.			
8 The individual members understand their roles and responsibilities properly and address them.			
9 The decisions are made by the whole group collectively and through compromise.			
10 We trust each other.			
11 Everybody's skills and strengths are exploited to the full.			
12 Every person feels a valued member of the group.			
13 We regularly review our progress using our Gantt chart.			
14 All the group members appear to be committed to the group goals.			
15 We are on track with our tasks.			
16 We review our team goals regularly.			
17 We have the skills that we need within our group to complete our tasks and achieve our goals.			
18 We have the resources that we need to complete our tasks and achieve our goals.			

What changes do we want to make to improve our group work?

1 _____

2 _____

3 _____

4 _____

Chapter 6, page 65

Peer evaluation form			
Student name: _____			
Role in group: _____			
Main responsibilities:	Peer reviewers' feedback		
	Always	S/times	Never
Attends group meetings			
Is well prepared for group meetings			
Listens to group members and shows respect for what they say			
Contributes to meetings by giving ideas			
Offers help to group members when they need it			
Is open-minded to suggestions and is prepared to compromise			
Has completed the tasks assigned or is on track with them			
Is committed to the group goals			

Peer reviewers' comments

Things I would to thank this team member for:

_____

_____

_____

Things I would like my team member to think about:

_____

_____

_____

_____

Reflection on my peers' comments:

1 _____

2 _____

3 _____

4 _____

Chapter 6, page 67

Goal review form			
Goal	Still appropriate?	Achieved it or on track?	If not, why not? What needs to happen to get on track? Is there a new goal?
Goal 1			
Goal 2			
Goal 3			
Goal 4			
Goal 5			
Goal 6			
Goal 7			
Goal 8			

Chapter 7, page 71

Group dynamics evaluation form

As you watch the recording of your group work session, tick the appropriate column of the table for each of the seven aspects of behaviour. Add comments of your own.

	True	False	Don't know	Comments
1 One member of the group did most of the talking.				
2 All members of the group contributed to the discussion.				
3 Everybody was polite and respectful to everybody else.				
4 The decisions were arrived at through negotiation.				
5 Everybody did their fair share of the work.				
6 Everybody was present and on time for the meeting.				

Chapter 7, page 73

Task agreement form				
Group member	Task	Complete by	Agreed and signed by	Group feedback on the task

Chapter 7, page 74

Ground rule reminder

To group member: _____

In order to improve our group work, please remember the following ground rules:

1 _____

2 _____

3 _____

4 _____

Please let us know how we can support you in our group work.

Signed by your group members

Chapter 8, page 79

Presentation guidance form

Objectives

1 **What is the aim of the presentation?** (to describe / analyse / explain / explore / discuss …)

_____

Audience

2 Who is the audience?

_____

3 How much do they know already about the topic?

_____

4 What do they want to know?

_____

5 What do we want to tell them?

_____

Guidelines

6 How many people will present?

_____

7 How long should it last?

_____

8 How many slides should there be?

_____

9 Other points:

_____

Chapter 9, page 86

Writing assignment framework			
Section	Purpose and main ideas	Some sources referred to	Word count
Section 1:			
Section 2:			
Section 3:			
Section 4:			
Section 5:			
Section 6:			

Chapter 12, page 113

Group work evaluation form	
Evaluation of your group work performance	Comments
1 Did you start thinking about your assignment as soon as it was given to you?	
2 Did you spend some time thinking about the process of group work before you started on the actual assignment?	
3 Did you agree on ground rules at the start of your assignment?	
4 Did you allocate roles and responsibilities for your group members?	
5 Did you write a set of goals and objectives?	
6 Did you make a Gantt chart?	
7 Did you review your group's progress during the task?	
8 Did you review your performance during your group work?	
9 Did you review your group's performance during your group work?	
10 Did you give feedback to your group members about their work and performance during your group work?	
11 Did you meet your deadline comfortably?	
12 Were you happy with your mark for your group assignment?	
13 What skills did you improve during your group work?	
14 What subject knowledge did you improve during the presentation?	
15 What skills did you find that you need to improve?	
16 How could you improve the contribution you made to your group?	

Chapter 12, page 114

Skills audit review			
	Improvement made (what?)	No change (why not?)	(More) improvements needed in this area

Chapter 12, page 115

Skills and subject knowledge goals		
Skill area I want to improve	Time	Resources

Appendix 6 – Example group presentation

The following transcript is an example of a group presentation. The comments highlight the features that make this a good example of a group work assignment.

> **Example:** *Work in groups of three or four. Research, prepare and deliver a class presentation with the following title:*
>
> *'What are the advantages and disadvantages for students of being given group work assignments at university?'*
>
> *Refer to both secondary and primary research in your talk.*

Lise: *Hello, everyone, and thank you for coming to our presentation today. My name is Lise and I'll just ask my other group members to introduce themselves.*

Abdullah: *Hello, I'm Abdullah.*

Nurul: *My name's Nurul.*

Sam: *And I'm Sam.*

> **Comment:** It is a good idea to let everyone introduce themselves at the start of the presentation. It gives the immediate impression that you are a team and that you have worked together to prepare your talk.

Lise: *The subject of our presentation is the advantages and disadvantages of using group work for university students. As we've found out since we started studying here, group work is a popular way of giving work to students in this university. I think it's quite new to a lot of us who come from other countries where it's not used so much, and it has been very interesting and challenging – and it certainly has caused a lot of debate amongst us as students. First of all, me and Abdullah are going to talk about some of the advantages of group work and then after that, Nurul and Sam will be discussing the more challenging aspects of working in teams. So now I'll hand over to Abdullah, who is going to discuss the main advantage of group work.*

> **Comment:** Lise shows that she knows what her group members are going to talk about. By using their names and giving an outline of what they will say, she shows this is one cohesive presentation, not individual presentations by individual students.

Abdullah: *Thanks, Lise. Yes, as Lise says, I'm going to discuss what is probably the biggest benefit of group work, which is that it improves your teamwork skills. This is important because teamwork skills are essential in modern life. In almost any professional field of work, you'll have colleagues who you'll be required to work with and you'll need a wide variety of teamwork skills to do well in your job, so by doing group work now we are preparing ourselves for the world of work in the future. Recent research, notably studies by Stern et al in 2009 and Ridley in 2010, which you can read more about in the handout that Sam is giving out, shows that the ability to work and collaborate closely with colleagues is one of the most important qualities that employers look for in employees.*

Comment: As Abdullah talks, Sam supports him by passing round the handouts. This is an example of working together as a team.

Abdullah: *(continues) … And what are the best ways of developing teamwork skills? Well, you won't be surprised to hear that there's a broad consensus amongst educationalists that you learn and develop teamwork skills by doing group work – by working through group tasks in which you have to work with others, share your ideas and knowledge, collaborate, negotiate, support others, ask and offer help, meet deadlines, and so on. I'd just like to say that in our team we had some disagreements about how to approach this presentation. In fact, we had a small argument, and I admit I was involved, but then I realized that it was more important to carry on working together than to win the argument. So we all agreed to compromise, and later I realized that my group member was probably right about what she was saying, so I certainly improved my group work skills through working on this assignment.*

Comment: Abdullah comments on problems that his group faced and how they were resolved. This shows that he has learned from his experience of group work.

Abdullah: *(continues) … So that's the first main point of our presentation: that giving students group work develops their teamwork skills, which are essential life skills. So now Lise is going to carry on discussing some of the other benefits of working in groups at university.*

Comment: Abdullah hands over to the next group member and says what she will talk about. This is another example of good group work.

Group Work

Lise: *Thanks, Abdullah. Yes, although as Abdullah says 'teamwork skills' is what everyone thinks of when they think about group work, there are a number of other positive outcomes of working in groups. One of these is that you can learn a lot more about your subject if you work in a group than if you work alone. This is because you can pool your ideas. In a good group discussion, in which you have to give your opinion on an issue and defend it, you really get to see an issue from all different angles, so it could be argued that group work gives you a better, more thorough, deeper understanding of topic knowledge than working individually does. When we were preparing for this presentation, it was my job to collect ideas about the advantages of group work. I thought I had done a good job, but when I presented my ideas in a group meeting, all my group members came up with some more ideas that I hadn't come across, so it really became clear to me that you can share knowledge and come up with more things than you can think of individually.*

Comment: By referring to a group discussion that they had while they were preparing their presentation, Lise shows that her group collaborated on their assignment.

Lise: *(continues) ... Group work is also good for weaker students because they can get the support of more able students, and you could also argue that stronger students themselves benefit as well from giving support to weaker students. I do acknowledge that differing levels of abilities in groups can be a challenge – something which Nurul will say more about – but there are positive sides to it as well.*

Comment: Lise mentions something that a member of her group will talk about later. This shows that they have worked together to prepare the presentation.

Lise: *(continues) ... My final point is that group work can be very motivating for students. Individual work can be dull, boring, sitting on your own. Many students enjoy the motivation of group work, which tends to be more active and dynamic than individual work. I know I'm one of those students who like to be active in their learning! OK, so we've talked about many of the benefits of group work, and now it's time for Nurul and Sam to discuss the challenging aspects of this issue.*

Comment: This is another good example of an effective handover to the next group member.

Nurul: *Thank you, Lise. I'm going to start this part of the presentation by talking about one of the main negative points about group work, which is the difficulty of assessing it, and afterwards Sam will carry on with another major challenge of group work.*

Comment: This is another good example of referring to something that another group member will discuss later.

Nurul: (continues) ... *As I said, one of the main drawbacks about group work is how to assess it – the issue being that students in the same group are usually given the same mark, and this mark might not reflect the amount of work done by each of the students or the ability of each of the students, and this can have a serious impact on student motivation, as well as just not being fair. When a group hands in a group assignment or gives a group presentation, it might not be very clear to the marker who has done most of the work. It's obviously not fair if one student hasn't done any work but gets a good mark. We surveyed students on our programme – I surveyed year one students, Sam did second year students and Lise and Abdullah did year three students – and then we pooled and analysed our results.*

Comment: Nurul talks about the research their group did. She shows how they divided up the work and then pooled their findings. This demonstrates how well they worked together as a group.

Nurul: (continues) ... *We found that the majority of the students we asked felt that group work marks did not fairly reflect the amount of work that individual students had done on the assignment. This can result in students being demotivated, and it can also lead to bad feeling between students. In some cases, lecturers give individual marks and group marks for a group assignment, but even then the group work element might not be very fair. Now it's over to Sam to talk about another challenge of group work.*

Comment: This is another good example of a handover to the next speaker.

Sam: *OK, thanks very much, Nurul, and Lise and Abdullah as well. As Nurul said, I'm going to talk about another big challenge of group work and then I'm going to wrap up the presentation with a conclusion. My point is related to what Nurul said about students all being different and some not working as hard as others or not having the same ability as other students.*

Comment: By referring to what his team member said, Sam shows this is one continuous and cohesive presentation.

Group Work

Sam: (continues) … *My concern is that some people might be held back by other students who are simply not doing the work properly, either because they find it too hard or because they're too lazy. Group tasks often require one student to complete their task before others can do their bit, so a keen student might not get the chance to do their bit well if they have to wait too long for the other students to do their work. This could result in hard-working students getting lower marks than they would in individual assignments. It might mean that good learning opportunities are wasted and that students don't learn very much. This could be very frustrating and demotivating for students and could deny them the educational opportunities they're paying for because, as you know, we all pay fees for our studies. Nurul mentioned a survey that we carried out. This showed that a substantial number of students had experienced frustration with other team members for not pulling their weight during group work assignments.*

Comment: This is another reference to what another group member has said.

Sam: (continues) … *OK, so that brings us to the conclusion of our presentation. Lise and Abdullah talked about the importance of developing teamwork skills and improving your subject knowledge through working in groups, and Nurul and I talked about the problems of assessment and some students being held back by other students.*

Comment: Here are more references to things that group members have talked about.

Sam: (continues) … *The teamwork argument is a strong one: we do need teamwork skills in the modern world and the only way to develop them is through teamwork itself. For that reason, lecturers are right to give us group work. However, we, as students, believe that lecturers need to be very careful how they award marks for group work, and that where possible students should be given individual marks which reflect their individual personal achievement and how much work they have done. So we'd like to thank you for listening to our presentation.*

Nurul: *Thank you.*

Lise: *Thanks.*

Abdullah: *Thanks a lot. Now we'd like to offer you the opportunity to ask questions and we'll do our best to answer them.*

Comment: All the group members say something at the end of the presentation to emphasize their group membership.

Glossary

Some of the more difficult words from the chapters are defined here in this Glossary. The definitions focus on the meanings of the words in the context in which they appear in the text. Definitions are from *COBUILD Advanced Dictionary*.

Key

ADJ	adjective	N-UNCOUNT	uncount noun
ADV	adverb	N-VAR	variable noun
AUX	auxiliary verb	NEG	negative
COLOUR	colour word	NUM	number
COMB	combining form	ORD	ordinal
CONJ	conjunction	PASSIVE	see V-PASSIVE
CONVENTION	convention	PHRASAL VERB	phrasal verb
DET	determiner	PHRASE	phrase
EXCLAM	exclamation	PREDET	predeterminer
FRACTION	fraction	PREFIX	prefix
LINK	see V-LINK	PREP	preposition
MODAL	modal verb	PRON	pronoun
N-COUNT	count noun	QUANT	quantifier
N-PLURAL	plural noun	QUEST	question word
N-PROPER	proper noun	SUFFIX	suffix
N-PROPER-PLURAL	plural proper noun	VERB	verb
N-SING	singular noun	V-LINK	link verb
N-TITLE	title noun	V-PASSIVE	passive verb

a

academic register (academic registers) N-VAR
Academic register of a piece of speech or writing is the level and style of language that is used in a university context.

adequately ADV
If something is done adequately, it is done well enough to be used or accepted.

adjourn (adjourns, adjourning, adjourned) VERB
If a meeting or trial is adjourned, or it adjourns, it is stopped for a short time.

admit (admits, admitting, admitted) VERB
If you admit that something bad, unpleasant, or embarrassing is true, you agree, often unwillingly, that it is true.

agenda (agendas) N-COUNT
An agenda is a list of items that have to be discussed at a meeting.

aim (aims) N-COUNT
The aim of something that you do is the purpose for which you do it or the result that it is intended to achieve.

allocate (allocates, allocating, allocated) VERB
If one item or share of something is allocated to a person or for a particular purpose, it is given to that person or used for that purpose.

anticipate (anticipates, anticipating, anticipated) VERB
If you anticipate an event, you realize in advance that it will happen.

appoint (appoints, appointing, appointed) VERB
If you appoint someone to a job or official position, you choose them for it.

appreciate (appreciates, appreciating, appreciated) VERB
If you appreciate something, you like it because you recognize its good qualities.

approachable ADJ
If you describe someone as approachable, you think that they are friendly and easy to talk to.

arise (arises, arising, arose, arisen) VERB
If a situation or problem arises, it begins to exist or people begin to become aware of it.

assign (assigns, assigning, assigned) VERB
If you assign a piece of work to someone, you give them the work to do.

assignment (assignments) N-COUNT
An assignment is a task or piece of work that you are given to do, especially as part of your job or studies.

available ADJ
If something you want or need is available, you can find it or obtain it.

b

background reading N-UNCOUNT
Background reading involves the reading of related works in order to get extra information on a topic that you are intending to study or write about.

beneficial ADJ
Something that is beneficial helps people or improves their lives.

brainstorm (brainstorms, brainstorming, brainstormed) VERB
If a group of people brainstorm, they have a meeting in which they all put forward as many ideas and suggestions as they can think of.

c

capacity N-UNCOUNT
The capacity of something such as a factory or airport is the quantity of things it can produce or deal with using the equipment or resources that are available.

cohesive ADJ
Something that is cohesive consists of parts that fit together well and form a united whole.

collaborate (collaborates, collaborating, collaborated) VERB
When one person or group participates with another, they work together, especially on a book or on some research.

collate (collates, collating, collated) VERB
When you collate pieces of information, you gather them all together and examine them.

collusion N-UNCOUNT
Collusion is secret or illegal cooperation, especially between countries or organizations.

comfort zone (comfort zones) N-COUNT
If you are in your comfort zone, you are in a situation or position in which you feel secure, comfortable, or in control.

commit to (commits to, committing to, committed to) VERB
If you commit yourself to something, you say that you will definitely do it.

common practice N-UNCOUNT
Common practice is a generally accepted way of doing something.

compromise (compromises) N-VAR
A compromise is a situation in which people accept something slightly different from what they really want, because of circumstances or because they are considering the wishes of other people.

consensus N-SING
A consensus is general agreement among a group of people.

consequence (consequences) N-COUNT
The consequence of something are the results or effects of it.

consistent ADJ
Someone who is consistent always behaves in the same way, has the same attitude to people or things, or achieves the same level of success in something.

constraint (constraints) N-COUNT
A constraint is something that limits or controls what you can do.

convenient ADJ
If a way of doing something is convenient, it is done in a way that is useful or suitable for you.

cope (copes, coping, coped) VERB
If you cope with a problem or task, you deal with it successfully.

core text (core texts) N-COUNT
Core texts are the texts that have to be studied on a university course.

critical thinking N-UNCOUNT
Critical thinking is an active and careful consideration of a belief and the evidence to support it.

cue card (cue cards) N-COUNT
Cue cards are cards with notes written on them to remind a speaker of what they want to say during a presentation or speech.

d

deadline (deadlines) N-COUNT
A deadline is a time or date before which a particular task must be finished or a particular thing must be done.

deadlock (deadlocks) N-VAR
If a dispute or series of negotiations reaches deadlock, no agreement can be reached because neither side will give in at all.

delivery N-UNCOUNT
You talk about someone's delivery when you are referring to the way they give a speech or lecture.

distinction (distinctions) N-COUNT
If you make a distinction you say two things are different.

distraction (distractions) N-COUNT
A distraction is something that turns your attention away from something you want to concentrate on.

distribute (distributes, distributing, distributed) VERB
If you distribute things, you hand them or deliver them to a number of people.

e

effective ADJ
Something that is effective works well and produces the results that were intended.

emerge (emerges, emerging, emerged) VERB
If a fact or problem emerges from a period of thought, discussion, or investigation, it becomes known as a result of it.

emphasis (emphases) N-VAR
Emphasis is special or extra importance that is given to an activity or to a part or aspect of something.

enable (enables, enabling, enabled) VERB
If someone or something enables you to do a particular thing, they give you the opportunity to do it.

enhance (enhances, enhancing, enhanced) VERB
To enhance something means to improve its value, quality, or attractiveness.

evaluate (evaluates, evaluating, evaluated) VERB
If you evaluate something or someone, you consider them in order to make a judgement about them.

expand (expands, expanding, expanded) VERB
If something such as an organization or service expands, it becomes larger.

exploit (exploits, exploiting, exploited) VERB
If you exploit something, you use it well, and achieve something or gain an advantage from it.

f

face (faces, facing, faced) VERB
If you face something difficult or unpleasant, it is going to affect you and you have to deal with it.

faction (factions) N-COUNT
A faction is an organized group within another group which opposes some of the ideas of the larger group and fights for its own ideas.

feasible ADJ
if something is feasible, it can be done, made, or achieved.

fluency N-UNCOUNT
Someone who can speak a language with fluency can speak it easily and correctly.

formulate (formulates, formulating, formulated) VERB
If you formulate something such as a plan or proposal, you invent it, thinking about the details carefully.

forum (forums) N-COUNT
A forum is a place, situation, or group in which people exchange ideas and discuss issues, especially important public issues.

framework (frameworks) N-COUNT
A framework is a particular set of rules, ideas, or beliefs which you use in order to deal with problems or decide what to do.

fundamental ADJ
If one thing is fundamental to another, it is absolutely necessary to it, and the second thing cannot exist, succeed, or be imagined without it.

g

Gantt chart (Gantt charts) N-COUNT
A Gantt chart is a type of bar chart showing the progress of activity planned to take place during specified periods.

ground rule (ground rules) N-COUNT
The ground rules for something are the basic principles on which future action will be based.

group dynamics N-PLURAL
The dynamics of a situation or group of people are the opposing forces within it that cause it to change.

h

hinder (hinders, hindering, hindered) VERB
If something hinders you, it makes it more difficult for you to do something or make progress.

hindsight N-UNCOUNT
Hindsight is the ability to understand and realize something about an event after it has happened, although you did not understand or realize it at the time.

hub (hubs) N-COUNT
A hub or a hub airport is a large airport from which you can travel to other airports.

i

ice-breaker (ice-breakers) N-COUNT
An ice-breaker is something that someone says or does in order to make it easier for people who have never met before to talk to each other.

in depth ADV
If you deal with a subject in depth, you deal with it thoroughly and consider all the aspects of it.

inadequacy N-UNCOUNT
If someone has feelings of inadequacy, they feel that they do not have the qualities and abilities necessary to do something or cope with life in general.

inflexible ADJ
Something that is inflexible cannot be altered in any way, even if the situation changes.

infrastructure (infrastructures) N-VAR
The infrastructure of a country, society, or organization consists of the basic facilities such as transport, communications, power supplies, and buildings, which enable it to function.

insecure ADJ
If you are insecure, you lack confidence because you think you are not good enough or not loved.

insist (insists, insisting, insisted) VERB
If you insist that something should be done, you say so very firmly and refuse to give in about it.

intense ADJ
Intense is used to describe something that is very great or extreme in strength or degree.

interactive ADJ
If you describe a group of people or their activities interactive, you mean that the people communicate with each other.

intonation (intonations) N-VAR
Your intonation is the way your voice rises and falls as you speak.

intuition (intuitions) N-VAR
Your intuition or your intuitions are unexplained feelings you have that something is true even when you have no evidence or proof of it.

investment N-UNCOUNT
Investment of time or effort is the spending of time or effort on something in order to make it a success.

j

justify (justifies, justifying, justified) VERB
To justify a decision, action, or idea, is to show that it is reasonable or necessary.

l

learning outcome (learning outcomes) N-COUNT
A learning outcome is what a student is expected to know, understand, or be able to demonstrate at the end of a period of study.

learning style (learning styles) N-COUNT
Learning styles are the different methods that students use to learn and their particular approaches to studying.

m

methodology (methodologies) N-VAR
A methodology is a system of methods and principles for doing something, for example for carrying out research.

monitor (monitors, monitoring, monitored) VERB
If you monitor something, you regularly check its development or progress, and sometimes comment on it.

mull over (mulls over, mulling over, mulled over) VERB
if you mull something over, you think about it for a long time before deciding what to do.

n

negotiate (negotiates, negotiating, negotiated) VERB
If people negotiate with each other, they talk about a problem or a situation such as a business arrangement in order to solve the problem or complete the arrangement.

nominate (nominates, nominating, nominated) VERB
If someone is nominated for a job or position, you formally choose them to hold that job or position.

norm N-SING
If you say a situation is the norm, you mean that it is usual and expected.

o

objective ADJ
If someone is objective, they base their opinions on facts rather than on their personal feelings.

objective (objectives) N-COUNT
Your objective is what you are trying to achieve.

offence (offences) N-COUNT
An offence is a crime that breaks a particular law and requires a particular punishment.

on track PHRASE
If someone or something is on track, they are acting or progressing in a way that is likely to result in success.

option (options) N-COUNT
An option is something that you can choose to do in preference to one or more alternatives.

overcome (overcomes, overcoming, overcame) VERB
If you overcome a problem or a feeling, you successfully deal with it and control it.

p

participate (participates, participating, participated) VERB
If you participate, you take part in something.

participation N-UNCOUNT
Your participation in an activity is when you take part in it.

peer (peers) N-COUNT
Your peers are the people who have the same age as you or have the same status as you.

penalise (penalises, penalising, penalised) VERB
If a person or group is penalised for something, they are made to suffer in some way because of it.

penalty (penalties) N-COUNT
A penalty is a punishment that someone is given for doing something that is against a law or rule.

persist (persists, persisting, persisted) VERB
if something undesirable persists, it continues to exist.

placement (placements) N-COUNT
If someone who is training gets a placement, they get a job for a period of time to give them experience in the job they are training for.

portal (portals) N-COUNT
On the Internet, a portal is a site that consists of links to other websites.

preconception (preconceptions) N-COUNT
Your preconceptions about something are your beliefs formed about it before you have enough information or experience.

preliminary ADJ

Preliminary activities or discussions take place at the beginning of an event, often as a form of preparation.

proactive ADJ

Proactive actions are intended to cause changes, rather than just reacting to change.

promote (promotes, promoting, promoted) VERB

If people promote something, they help or encourage it to happen or spread.

r

random ADJ

A random sample or method is one in which all the people or things involved have an equal chance of being chosen.

reasoning (reasonings) N-VAR

Reasoning is the process by which you reach a conclusion after thinking about all the facts.

reference (references) N-COUNT

A reference is a word, phrase, or idea which comes from something such as a book, poem, or play, and which you use when making a point about something.

refine (refines, refining, refined) VERB

If something such as a process, theory, or machine is refined, it is improved by having small changes made to it.

reflective ADJ

If you are reflective, you are thinking deeply about something.

representative ADJ

A group of people or things is representative of a larger group of people or things if it closely matches the wider group.

resource (resources) N-COUNT

The resources of an organization or person, are the materials, money, and other things that they have and can use in order to function properly.

restriction (restrictions) N-COUNT

A restriction is an official rule that limits what you can do or limits the amount or size of something.

rework (reworks, reworking, reworked) VERB

If you rework something such as an idea or piece of writing, you reorganize it and make changes to it in order to improve it or bring it up to date.

ridicule (ridicules, ridiculing, ridiculed) VERB

If you ridicule someone or ridicule their ideas or beliefs, you make fun of them in an unkind way.

s

significant ADJ

A significant amount or effect is large enough to be important or affect a situation to a noticeable degree.

signposting ADJ

Signposting words and phrases show how ideas are connected in a spoken or written text, and help the listener or reader follow the text.

skills audit (skills audits) N-COUNT

A skills audit is a thorough check or examination of a person's skills and abilities.

stimulate (stimulates, stimulating, stimulated) VERB

To stimulate something means to encourage it to begin or develop further.

storm (storms) N-COUNT

If something causes a storm, it causes an angry or violent reaction from a large number of people.

strategy (strategies) N-COUNT

A strategy is a plan or set of plans intended to achieve something, especially over a long period.

struggle (struggles, struggling, struggled) VERB

If you are struggling to do something, you are trying hard to do it, even though other people or things may be making it difficult to succeed.

submission N-UNCOUNT

The submission of a proposal, report, or other document is the act of formally sending it to someone, so that they can consider it or decide about it.

superficial ADJ

If you describe something such as an action, feeling, or relationship as superficial, you mean it includes only the simplest and most obvious aspects of that thing.

sustainable ADJ
You use sustainable to describe the use of natural resources when this use is kept at a steady level that is not likely to damage the environment.

t

tackle (tackles, tackling, tackled) VERB
If you tackle a problem or difficult task, you deal with it in a very determined or efficient way.

tolerate (tolerates, tolerating, tolerated) VERB
If you tolerate a situation or person, you accept them although you do not particularly like them.

trust N-UNCOUNT
Your trust in someone is your belief that they are honest and sincere and will not deliberately do anything to harm you.

v

victimise (victimises, victimising, victimised) VERB
If someone is victimised, they are deliberately treated unfairly.

virtual learning environment (VLE) (virtual learning environments) N-COUNT
A VLE is an education system based on the web that models real-world education by providing equivalent web access to things such as classes, class content, tests, and other external resources.

vital ADJ
If you say something is vital, you mean that it is necessary or very important.

w

water-cooler chat (water cooler chats) N-COUNT
A water-cooler chat refers to the informal conversations that people have in their office or workplace around the water cooler.

weigh up (weighs up, weighing up, weighed up) VERB
If you weigh someone up, you try and find out what they are like and form an opinion of them, especially when you are suspicious of them.

well-suited ADJ
If something is well suited to a particular purpose, it is right or appropriate for that purpose.

wiki (wikis) N-COUNT
A wiki is a website that allows anyone visiting it to change or add to the material in it.

Answer key

Chapter 1

The purpose of the quiz is to get you thinking about your own beliefs before you start reading the chapter. The comments on the quiz provide information on how colleges and universities in the West would normally view these issues.

As these issues will be dealt with in the rest of each chapter, you do not need to spend too much time thinking about the comments and how they affect you. However, it would be useful to revisit the quiz when you finish each chapter to see if your opinion has changed.

Quiz self-evaluation

1 Sometimes you will *have to* work as part of a team even if you would prefer not to. If you find it hard to work with others, this book will help you to understand the value of group work and give you advice to make it as easy as possible.

2 You need to be flexible so that you can work as part of a team when you need to, but can also work on your own when that is more appropriate.

3 If every student expected the others to follow what they said, the group would have serious problems. It is important to listen to other students and make any necessary compromises.

4 At English-speaking universities your lecturers believe that you can learn a lot from other students. Other students might disagree with you and ask you to explain your opinions; this is an important part of the learning process.

5 Your lecturers certainly believe this. You should always listen carefully to what other students say as this will encourage you to question your own ideas and prompt you to do more background reading or discuss issues with your lecturer.

6 English universities consider group work activity as a very important part of the learning process. The lecturer may be more interested in how you

work as part of a group than in looking at the final piece of work.

Note: Each time you check the answers and/or read the comments, take time to reflect on what you have read.

■ Do you find the information useful or interesting?

■ Have you changed your mind about anything?

■ How do you feel this relates to the success of your future studies?

Exercise 1

1 **English-speaking universities:** True
Your own country: If false, you will need to work through this book particularly carefully to understand the aims and value of group work. Working with other students is an important part of learning in English-speaking universities.

2 **English-speaking universities:** True
Your own country: If false, you need to understand that you will have to put in extra time with other students outside class and understand why it is important to do so.

3 **English-speaking universities:** True
Your own country: If false, you will need to learn the *value* of working with others.

4 **English-speaking universities:** True
Your own country: If false, you will have to learn how to listen to and learn from other students. It is important to understand that your lecturer will expect you to do this.

5 **English-speaking universities:** True
Your own country: Taking responsibility for your learning might be new for you. If so, you will need all the help and support you can get. Group work can provide you with a lot of the support you need.

Exercise 2

In all these tasks you can probably achieve more by working in a group. You can share your ideas and skills and take the best ideas from the group without relying just on your own resources. The group can also allocate tasks to the student with the most appropriate skills, and, in this way learn even more from each other. Furthermore, by dividing up the work, you can deal with each area in more depth.

Exercise 3

1 This is a very **good group** work task. You would need to collaborate with other students, using a wide variety of teamwork skills, including sharing ideas, making suggestions, allocating tasks, helping each other, persuading, learning from and listening to others.

2 **Individual work**. This is a clearly a very personalized task. However, you may still benefit from discussing with others how they go about the task.

3 This is probably more suitable for **individual work** although it may be possible to do this with a student from the same country as you. It might be particularly useful to get one or more students to help you with research.

4 This is a good **group work** task, and it would use a wide variety of teamwork skills similar to those in task 1. Such activities require ideas, and it is usually best to generate these from a wide variety of people before choosing which ones to make use of.

5 This is clearly **individual work**. You would need to write this in a way that relates to your own experience. However, once again, it can be useful to discuss ideas with other students.

Chapter 2

Quiz self-evaluation

1 Most students like to choose their own group members, but often you do not have the choice. You need to be willing to work with anybody you are asked to and develop ways of getting on with a variety of people.

2 This may be true, but you often learn more when you have to do things that are more challenging

or even difficult. By overcoming problems, you are likely to learn more.

3 It is not *always* necessary to do team-building activities. However, if you do not know your team members and need to build trust, then team-building activities can be very helpful.

4 Rules might not be necessary if you have the ideal group with excellent team members that all get along together. However, this is rarely the case, and rules are needed to keep things on track and stop misunderstandings.

5 Although group members should help each other, they often need encouragement to do so. Having individual responsibilities discourages group members from avoiding work.

Exercise 1

1 **Advantages:** It is a quick way to choose the group. There are no arguments about who the group members will be. Everybody is treated the same and no students are left without a group. The lecturer can also make sure that the groups are balanced and have a good mix of abilities, nationalities and gender.

   Disadvantages: The students might feel they do not have the right or power to make their own decisions. The lecturer might not be aware of difficulties between some of the students. The students might resent the lecturer putting them into a particular group.

2 **Advantages:** Students can choose other students who they get along with. They have a feeling of ownership over their group.

   Disadvantages: Some students might not easily find a group, and this might make them uncomfortable. It might not be the best option when doing serious work for students to choose their friends. Also, group members might end up being very similar, for example, the same gender or the same nationality, so the group may miss out on different viewpoints.

3 **Advantages:** The lecturer can make sure the group is well balanced, with a good mix of nationalities and gender. Students enjoy having some control over their group membership and may respond well to this.

Disadvantages: Some students might not easily find a group and this might make them feel uncomfortable.

4 **Advantages:** It is quick and easy. There are no arguments. You cannot blame anybody if the group does not work together well. It is considered fair because everyone has the same chance of who they will work with.

Disadvantages: You might have all the best students in the same group, and some groups might have all the weak students. You might have students who find it difficult to work together in the same group (although this might also be a good thing).

Exercise 2

1 Team members will probably want to know how to pronounce this name as well as how to spell it. Make sure you get it right as names are important.

2 Team members might want to know why Narantuya uses a different name at university and how she chose it.

3–4 Team members might not know about all the different cultures, languages and ethnic groups in China. They might want to know a bit more about these things and this might be a good opportunity to improve everyone's general knowledge.

5 Team members will almost certainly want to know what other languages Natalie speaks, and when she uses Mongolian and Mandarin.

6 Team members might want to know why Natalie moved from her home region to Shanghai.

7 Team members will know that Natalie is studying Mechanical Engineering if they are all on the same course. However, they will probably ask why, which will lead to the next question.

8 Team members might be interested in what other subjects are popular and the chance of getting jobs in the chosen discipline.

9 Team members probably do not associate horse riding with the Chinese, and this is an opportunity to talk a bit about Mongolian culture. They might be interested in finding out where Natalie has travelled and what places she is planning to visit.

10 This might provoke a discussion about renewable energy, its potential in China and how Natalie sees the future of energy use and production.

Exercise 3

The following is a commentary on the value of the eight different skills and the value they can have in a group. By reading this commentary you can evaluate your own value in a group and what skills you might want to improve.

1 A student with good skills in this area would be very useful as the group secretary. Having such a person in the group would not only help keep a good record of discussions and decisions, but also be a good model for students that are weaker in this area.

2 It is useful to have a group that has many members with good skills in this area. However, good speakers should ideally be good listeners as well, not only so they do not dominate the group, but so they can also reformulate what weaker speakers have to say.

3 This is important for all members of the group and something all students should work on. There are many misunderstandings caused by mispronunciation, not just about content, but also how the student comes across, whether as dominating or accommodating, polite or impolite.

4 This is something that all group members should work on as presentations sometimes have to be given individually. However, having someone who is good at presentations within the group can be a very good source of help to other group members, both for passing on techniques and helping to develop confidence.

5 This is a more specialized area, and will usually be a skill that only some students excel in. A good IT specialist is a real asset to the group, and can save a lot of time that would otherwise be spent using IT inappropriately or without proper understanding.

6 Like IT skills, this is a skill that only some members will have. It will save a lot of time if you have someone who is good with numbers in your group.

7 Teamwork skills are something that all members should develop, so if yours are poor, then you need to learn how to improve them quickly.

8 Reading and note-taking is another very important university skill. However, some students will always be better at this, and having a good researcher in your group is an important asset, especially if they can summarize information in note form.

Exercise 4

1 Such activities are not difficult to complete, but it is easy to put them off. Most people need a reason to do such things, and having to discuss the answers in a group is usually enough motivation.

2 You can only really judge this by doing it yourself (see below).

3 You have probably already experienced sharing information with others. The only real problem is finding common experiences to share, and such activities will provide that. Some people are not keen on sharing experiences, and should not be pushed too much in an introductory meeting.

Doing the activity

Not everyone is good at reflection, so it is yet another skill you might need to develop. Take time to think quietly about the experiences mentioned in this activity. You should not try too hard, but just let your ideas flow. You may find it easier if you go for a walk, talk on a voice recorder, or think while listening to music. Whatever you do, try to remember how you felt in these different situations. You will find that your previous experiences are a very valuable resource and well worth thinking about.

Exercise 5

Like reflection, it is useful to think about situations that may happen in the future. When you are attending university, people will expect you to come up with ideas and solutions. If you have thought

about things in advance, it will make this process easier. Use this activity to try and imagine how the proposed solutions would work, and perhaps come up with some different ideas.

1 This could be an excellent way to learn about each other's customs and share recipes. It is a particularly good activity because it involves doing something practical and having something to show for it. Make sure that you will be happy to eat each other's food.

2 This could be fun and everyone would meet on neutral ground where there are distractions – and this can be much easier. However, some group members might not be interested or think going to the zoo is childish.

3 Like a zoo visit, this could be fun and has the benefit of being on neutral ground with distractions. However, some people are not keen on theme parks. It is important to find a destination that everyone is happy with and one that keeps people entertained when they are there.

4 This has the potential to be an excellent team-building activity as you might find out naturally how people take on different roles and responsibilities. People who are not keen might find it more rewarding than they had expected.

Exercise 6

1 The group chair needs to have leadership skills. He/She needs to be have an overview of the progress being made on the project. This person needs to be well-organized and sensitive, fair but firm.

2 The designer and developer needs to have hands-on experience of designing products. This person requires vision and drawing skills. He/She needs to have the practical ability to build the product using a range of materials and resources.

3 The marketing and publicity officer needs to be creative and have a good knowledge of advertising.

4 The accountant needs to have good maths skills and be very thorough. This person needs to be prepared to spend time checking details to make sure everything is correct.

5 The IT officer should have excellent IT skills and be able to work with a range of computer programmes to support the other members of the group.

Exercise 7

The spread of skills within any group will never be a perfect match. The skills within the group in Exercise 7 are quite broad, but it is not always clear who should take on particular roles. You might find that a person has a variety of skills and wishes to make use of one of their less obvious ones. There may also be clashes between group members for particular roles. This should always be dealt with sensitively.

1 Fatimah would make a good IT officer with her IT skills, especially as she is able to use them in a practical way. She also has business skills, and so she might make a good accountant. She might even be able to make use of skills she has learned doing photography and be a good designer and developer.

2 David is clearly a practical person and might make a good designer and developer. He has an interest in working with his hands and the ability to build and adapt things.

3 Lora might make a good group chair. She is popular and people seem to respect her; these are important assets in a chair. She would probably be good at solving any difficulties between group members.

4 Jinjie would probably make a good accountant with her maths and science background. She also has practical experience with spreadsheets and other software packages used for figures. On the other hand, she might be better suited as the IT officer.

5 Eduardo might be the best candidate for the post of marketing and publicity officer. He could create advertisements and publicity materials using his skills in graphic design and computers. On the other hand, he might be a candidate for the role of designer and developer.

Exercise 8

The following rules are suggestions. You might wish to write them differently.

1 All students must attend every meeting and arrive on time.

2 Mobile phones must be switched off during meetings.

3 Everybody must contribute to meetings.

4 At the end of the meeting, the group chair will review a list of action points. The group secretary will write up and distribute the action points immediately after the meeting.

5 Students must indicate when they want to make a point. They should not be allowed to interrupt a speaker; they must wait until the speaker has finished making their point.

6 Students who fail to complete their work on time will be referred to the lecturer.

7 Group meetings are confidential: students must not tell other groups about the content of their meetings or the details of their work.

8 There will be a group vote to make decisions.

9 There will be a meeting at least once a week.

Chapter 3

Quiz self-evaluation

1 This approach might work when you are working on your own, but it will almost certainly cause problems when you work in a group.

2 The documents include some very important information that you will need when planning your assignments. You should look after them carefully and refer to them whenever you need to.

3 One of the best things about working in a group is sharing your ideas and building on the ideas of others. You will find you not only learn from others but are prompted to think of more ideas of your own.

4 With university assignments, you have a fixed finishing time for your work that cannot be changed. This means you need to understand that each stage of the process has to be completed by a certain time. If you do not follow a clear and planned procedure, you will let yourself down as well as your group.

5 Things will be much easier for you and your group if you adopt this approach. You should always be ready to change and adapt to circumstances.

Exercise 1

Some possible questions that you could write are included here, but you may have other ones as well:

1 Who will I work with?
  Can I choose my group members?

2 When does the brochure need to be finished by?
  Should it be in colour?
  How many pages should the brochure be?
  Which computer programmes are we expected to use?
  Should we print it on special paper?
  How many copies should we produce?

3 How long should the presentation be?
  Should we use PowerPoint in the presentation?
  Should we include advertising in the presentation?
  Does everyone have to talk in the presentation?
  Can we include video in the presentation?

4 What percentage of marks goes towards this assignment?
  How many marks are awarded for the brochure?
  How many marks are awarded for the presentation?
  What are marks awarded for exactly?

Exercise 2

If this is new to you, it is a good idea to use it for real issues in your life. In this way, you can discover the power of brainstorming for coming up with ideas. The most important aspect of brainstorming is being prepared to write down any ideas however silly they might be. It is in the next stage, when you evaluate ideas, that you can think more carefully about whether they are realistic or not.

Exercise 3

Task	Group member	Mon a.m.	Mon p.m.	Tue a.m.	Tue p.m.	Wed a.m.	Wed p.m.	Thur a.m.	Thur p.m.	Fri a.m.	Fri p.m.
Discuss and plan group assignment	All	✗									
Research part of university	Sarah		✗								
	Nou		✗								
	Fahad		✗								
Video Sarah's locations	Sarah and Nou			✗							
Write introductory script	Fahad			✗							
Video Nou's locations	Sarah and Nou				✗						
Research locations for opening shots	Fahad				✗						
Video opening shots for film	Sarah and Fahad					✗					
Video Fahad's locations	Sarah and Fahad						✗				
Nou	Work on the digital presentation						✗				
Editing	Everyone							✗			
Details of presentations	Everyone								✗		
Practise presentation	Everyone									✗	
Give presentation and show film	Everyone										✗

Exercise 4

There are many objectives that a group could write for this task. Here are some examples.

- Carry out research into good design practice and its important features.

- Carry out research into the nature of the city centre, its needs, its current style of architecture.

- Design an appropriate building for the city centre taking the research into account.

- Make a drawing of the building using an appropriate software package.

- Make a model of the building.

- Prepare a presentation to explain and justify the design.

- Deliver the presentation.

Chapter 4

Quiz self-evaluation

1 You will need to learn to listen to other group members if you are going to work well with them; interrupting all the time will simply generate bad feeling towards you. If you want to make a point, note it down so you can remember to bring it up when the other person has finished.

2 Group work is not about liking people. You need to be professional and treat the other group members with respect as colleagues. The aim is to have an effective group, not a group of friends.

3 When working in a group, you will sometimes have to go along with the group decision even if you do not agree with it. You might even find it refreshing to act as a different person in the group environment. It is normal to disagree with some decisions, but if you find you disagree with every decision, your group might be having a problem that you should discuss with your lecturer.

4 Being a good listener is a good life skill. However, you might not be as good a listener as you think. If you think you are not good at listening, you just need to use the group meetings to practise the skill.

5 It is not just a matter of chance. If you plan for your meetings, you are much more likely to have a *good* meeting

Exercise 1

1 Good. This will help both the individual student and the group.

2 Good. This will help group members to solve problems as they arise rather than leaving them until there is a real problem.

3 Poor. This is the opposite of point 2 and will just store up problems for later.

4 Good. By listening carefully you are encouraging them to speak and so providing the group with a more balanced view.

5 Poor. Some people take time to express themselves, and by preventing them from finishing you will never know what they really wanted to say.

6 Poor. This is impolite and will have a bad effect on the group. It will also prevent some group members from giving their opinions and coming up with ideas.

7 Good. It is useful for all group members to express their opinions, even if they are not accepted.

8 Poor. This might seem a good idea in the short term, but in the long term will cause many difficulties. Part of group work is learning how to collaborate, and being prepared to compromise is part of that process.

9 Poor. Making unkind remarks about others is not only bad behaviour, but could also be an indication of your own insecurity.

10 Poor. Trust is a very important aspect of group work and a lack of honesty will destroy trust.

11 Poor. This relates to point 10. If you do not take responsibility, the other group members will lose trust in you, and this will affect the group dynamic.

12 Poor. This shows a lack of respect for others and will have a bad effect on the group dynamic.

13 Good. This will not only help the struggling student and generate trust, but will also help you to deepen your understanding of the issues involved.

Think carefully about your own behaviour. You might not be aware of what you actually do. If you have a good relationship with the other students in your group, you can ask them about your behaviour and how others see you.

Exercise 2
1 B

2 B

3 D

4 D

5 B

6 D

7 B

8 D

9 A

10 D

Exercise 3
1 No: This is not a sensitive way to respond.

2 No: This does not show any real interest in the speaker.

3 Yes: This reassures the speaker and encourages them to continue.

4 Yes: This has a similar function to phrase 3.

5 No: This is a strongly worded criticism of what the speaker is saying.

6 Yes: Like phrases 3 and 4, this reassures the speaker and encourages them to continue.

7 No: This is a direct insult.

8 No: This is an interruption and you should wait till the speaker has finished.

9 Yes: This encourages the speaker to continue.

10 Yes: This is similar to phrase 9.

Exercise 4
1 I think …

2 What do the rest of you think?

3 I disagree with you.

4 Why do you think …? Why are you so keen on …?

5 Everybody loves … It's an opportunity to …

6 That's true.

7 Then we should try to …

8 I hadn't thought of it like that.

9 I wonder if we could …

10 I think we should … What about if we …? How about …?

Exercise 5
Stage 1: Forming, c

Stage 2: Storming, e

Stage 3: Norming, a

Stage 4: Performing, d

Stage 5: Adjourning, b

Chapter 5

Quiz self-evaluation
1 We *are* basically the same, but everyone's behaviour, values and beliefs are heavily influenced by the environment and culture they grew up in. This chapter will help you to understand how people from different cultures and backgrounds may think and behave differently from you.

2 This is not necessarily true. You need to appreciate that people have different skills as well as different abilities. Understanding these differences is key to being a good group member.

3 This is true of people who have the learning style of a *feeler*. It is important to feel that what you are doing is right, but you need to be able to justify what you are doing as well.

4 If this is true, then you are probably a *doer*. That is fine, but remember that other people in your group might have other personality types, so you should not be impatient with them.

5 Most people would agree with this, but it can be difficult to do in practice. Whatever you think, you will still find it useful to work through this chapter and think about the kind of role that would suit you.

Exercise 1

You might be surprised by the information about your learning style. It is important to reflect on what it tells you and how this might have had an impact on your past learning.

Make use of any information that is new to you to help you to learn and study more effectively.

Exercise 2

Your personality is another important factor in the way you learn, study and interact with others. You will look at the impact of your personality in group work in Exercise 3.

Exercise 3

It is important to reflect on your own view of yourself before checking what your score in Exercise 2 indicates. Reflection is a skill you will need to use when you are studying in a university environment. It will help you to develop as a person and improve your chances of success in your studies and future work.

Exercise 4

Doing this exercise will help the process of reflection and development.

Exercise 5

It is important to avoid making wide generalizations about how people may behave because of their background. The following comments are meant to help explain behaviour, not to predict it.

1 **Collectivist cultures:** Students may be less talkative, even in a small group. They may be reluctant to offer their opinion because they think their ideas might not be important for other people.

   Individualistic culture: Students may feel very comfortable talking in a group and putting

their opinion forward. They may feel that their opinion is of value and others should pay attention to it.

2 **Collectivist culture:** Students may be unwilling to speak out in front of the class without being asked. They may not be comfortable interrupting the teacher or asking questions. They may not be used to having a lot of people listen to them.

   Individualistic culture: Students may feel comfortable talking in front of a big group because this is encouraged in their culture. They may feel happy to ask the teacher questions and offer an opinion, even if it is not fully informed.

3 **Collectivist culture:** Students may not want to have a big debate about the problem. They may expect other students to sense the problem and understand what needs to be done to solve it without having a big discussion about it. They may also want to avoid conflict.

   Individualistic culture: Students may want to discuss the problem. They may think it is a good idea to have a discussion or even an argument to clear the air and to understand each other.

Chapter 6

Quiz self-evaluation

1 Everybody should think about their own performance before they think about the performance of other group members. There are always things that you can do to improve your performance, whoever you are and however talented you are.

2 It is true that you *might* have an effective team without having to work hard, but that is not usually the case. You usually get out of teamwork what you put into it. You need to be prepared to talk, negotiate, share and work hard to make your group a good one.

3 Many students will not want to comment on the performance of other group members, and if the group work goes well, you might not have to. But if a group member is underperforming, you may have to talk to them and this chapter will help to provide you with strategies to do that.

4 It can be useful to get on and do things. However, when you are part of a group, you have to go forward together. This means reviewing what you have done at certain stages of the process. You should be prepared to do this from time to time.

5 One of the advantages of group work is that you can usually ask for and offer help when it is needed. You do not need to struggle on your own if you have a group to help you.

Exercise 1

Take some time to think carefully about the questions and how you perform in your group; try to answer the questions truthfully. If you can, talk to people you work or study with, or have worked or studied with in the past, to share their thoughts about how you could improve your performance.

Exercise 2

The value of this exercise is in thinking about the implications of the evaluation and how you could improve the working of the group it describes. Try to think about what you could do without putting the blame on other group members. Think about how you could participate in any improvement.

Exercise 3

Reading and reflecting on what your group members think about your performance should provide you with ideas about how you can improve that performance. This process of receiving feedback so that you can reflect on your performance is an important part of group work. It does not usually feel good to be evaluated, especially when there is criticism of your behaviour. However, it can be one of the best ways of improving performance.

Exercise 4

Reviewing your goals is an important way to make sure that your group is on track with its group work. Depending on how long the group work lasts, you might need to review your goals a number of times.

Why might goals have changed?

When circumstances change, your group needs the flexibility to change its goals. You might find that as you work, you gain more knowledge and information and realize that some of your original goals were not very well thought out. You need the courage to make new goals if this happens.

What might have happened to the assignment if the group had not brought it back on track?

If you fail to review your goals, you might not notice that you have failed to do certain important things until it is too late. This could have a big impact on the final mark for your group project. If you do not review your goals, you might not realize that you are behind time until it is too late.

Chapter 7

Quiz self-evaluation

1 If you ignore problems, you are probably just storing them up for the future. You have to face up to issues as they arise; otherwise the problems are likely to continue and may get worse.

2 Some people might think that an argument is the worst thing that can happen. Other people might think an argument can help to get all the problems out in the open. In general, you should try to discuss problems openly without getting into an argument, but if one does break out, you should not feel you have failed. Sometimes an argument is an unavoidable part of the process of solving the problem before moving on.

3 This may be partly true, but a weak group member also has the most to learn. This is an opportunity for you to learn how to manage such situations. For example, if you have someone who is not good at sharing and negotiating, it is an opportunity for you to learn how to manage the situation and perhaps help this group member to learn new skills.

4 Unfortunately, this probably will not work because you get marks for *group work* not for good *individual work*. If you can show your lecturer how you supported your group members and how they learned from you, you will get a good mark.

Group Work

5 If you repeatedly go to your tutor or lecturer with minor problems, they might think that you cannot manage group work. But if you go to them with a serious problem that you have tried to deal with, but one that is still an issue that is interfering with your group work, then they will not think you have failed.

Exercise 1

Read these reasons with care: they are just suggestions to help you to think about what may be causing group work problems that you might experience.

1 Some students may lack confidence because of their English language skills. Or they may come from a culture where it is not usual to offer personal opinions regarding work. They may not feel their comments will be valued. Alternatively, they may just be very shy.

2 The dominant students probably have very confident personalities. These students may get impatient with other students who are less confident, so they speak more and more to keep the meetings going. They might not actually be trying to dominate the group, but simply feel they have to help the group to move on.

3 The students who miss the meetings might be avoiding them because they are not sure what they should be doing or what their tasks are. They might feel that their opinion is not valued. They might not be confident about their knowledge and skills, and they might think that they do not have a lot to offer the group.

4 These students might need support in their work. They might not understand what they have to do, or they might not have the skills required to do the task. They might also be having problems in their personal life. Of course they might just be rather lazy.

5 If it is difficult to contact students, they are probably avoiding group work. Maybe they do not know what to do, or maybe they are finding the work hard and need support.

6 There are usually a number of ways of achieving group tasks. This is why it can be hard to agree on the best one. The way you like to do things might not be better than others, just different.

7 Unfortunately, some people are not used to compromising, and might think they appear weak if they do. However, if they see other people compromising, this might help them to do so.

8 You might not have prepared well enough for the meeting. If you prepare a list of things to work on or discuss in advance, you should have plenty to talk about.

9 This problem may arise because you have not adequately discussed what you want the end product to be. If students are clear about the direction you all want to go in, they can usually understand what they have to do to achieve the end product.

Exercise 2
1 f 2 d 3 e 4 b 5 c 6 a

Exercise 3
1 False: Sometimes we have the impression that something is happening, but actually it is not. In this case, although Faiz appears to be talking a lot, it is not actually true, and this can be seen from the video. Once group members realize Faiz is not talking all the time, they will feel more comfortable with him.

2 False: Again, things are not what they seem. Although Alora is making a lot of noise, he is not actually making a contribution to the discussion. On the other hand, it might seem that Jane is not contributing because she is quiet, but on the video it is clear that she *is* contributing to the discussion.

3 True: Once again, the video shows that things are not as they first appear. Faiz has a way of speaking that can seem rude in some cultures, but it is clear from other aspects of his behaviour that he is actually polite and respectful. Over time, Faiz will probably learn English-speaking conventions of politeness as his language skills improve.

4 Don't know: This is not clear because there are two contradictory things happening. On the one hand, there is discussion. On the other, one student always seems to get his own way.

182

5 False: It is clear from the video that some students are not prepared, probably because they have not done the necessary research.

6 False: When you are busy, it is easy to forget what has happened. At the beginning of a meeting you might be busy with organizational things. At the end of the meeting you might be very involved in decisions. In both cases it is easy to miss a student leaving early or coming late.

Chapter 8

Quiz self-evaluation

1 There is a *big* difference between a group presentation and an individual presentation. Your lecturer wants to see what you have achieved as a *group* and is assessing your *group work*, not your individual abilities.

2 Sometimes lecturers give group *and* individual marks in a group presentation. Even if you only get a group mark, this reflects the aim of the assessment – to give you a mark for how well you work in a group.

3 This is true, but even stronger students get help and support in some aspects of their work from others in the group.

4 It is true that there is more opportunity for informal language in spoken situations than in writing. However, even during presentations colloquial language will often be inappropriate, and the correct academic register is generally required.

5 Unfortunately, this is sometimes true, but you can learn a lot about your subject and about how to give presentations from watching other students. Try to take an interest in the presentations of others both for your sake and the sake of the presenter. Also, try and make your presentation interesting!

6 A presentation is formal, but that does not mean it has to be solemn. You can smile and make a joke while still being formal.

Exercise 1

1 Bad practice: You should divide up the presentation, but not immediately. Spend time discussing the presentation first.

2 Bad practice: This will not get you a better mark because it does not show good group work.

3 Bad practice: This is not a good way of exploiting the strengths of all the students in the group.

4 Good practice: You can practise your part alone, but you should practise it together as well.

5–7 These are all examples of good practice.

8 Good practice: But make sure your presentation is cohesive.

9–10 These are both examples of good practice.

11 This probably depends on the length of the presentation. There is a danger that you will stop the flow of the presentation if you change speakers too often.

Exercise 2

This is a suggested order for the tasks, but there is some room for flexibility in the list.

1 Have a discussion about the objectives, audience and guidelines for the presentation.

2 Decide on the general topic.

3 Research the content.

4 Choose three or four points to focus on as the main parts of the presentation.

5 Prepare each of the main points with a focus and a clear argument.

6 Prepare the conclusion.

7 Prepare the introduction.

8 Make a digital presentation/a poster/visual aids/ hand-outs.

9 Write cue cards to use during the presentation.

10 Practise the presentation before you give it.

11 Prepare the room for the presentation.

Exercise 3

1 As a group

2 As an individual, but you should have made a group decision on what to research

3–4 As an individual

5 As a group

6 As an individual, but you should probably write your own cue cards so you can tailor them to your own needs

7 As an individual, but the group should decide on the main points together

8 As a group: this shows the audience you are working as a team

9 As a group

10 As a group

Chapter 9

Quiz self-evaluation

1 When you hand in your group assignment, it should be one cohesive piece of work. This chapter will help you to understand how you can work together to make your work read like one coherent assignment even though different students will be responsible for different parts.

2 You might be able to write without a plan when you are working on your own. However, when you are working in a group, this approach is unlikely to work well; you would end up with very different work from each group member.

3 Leaving your work to the last minute is not an option with group work. You have a responsibility to the other group members to complete your work in good time. You can then all check it and give each other feedback.

4 This chapter should help you to find more mistakes in your writing. This is a long process and will need practice over time. However, learning from each other should speed up the process.

5 Reflective writing is harder than it sounds. You need to be aware of what you are writing, and not just describing what happened. As this chapter shows, reflective writing is about analysis, not description.

Exercise 1

1 Write your first draft.

2 Proofread your work for grammar, spelling and punctuation mistakes.

3 Have a break.

4 Revise what you have written.

5 Share what you have written with your group.

6 Give feedback to group members on the content of their writing.

7 Revise your writing in the light of feedback from group members.

Exercise 2

Many students come from all over the world to study in the UK. There are many reasons for this, but they usually say that having a British degree will help them to find a good job in their country later on. Although some foreign students have a great time when they study abroad, others find it more difficult.

One of the main problems with studying in an English-speaking university is the different academic culture. In Western universities students are expected to critically analyse material, whereas in some cultures the main emphasis is on learning facts.

Another difficulty that students may face is in the area of the language. Students who have English as a second language have to learn how to express themselves in academic and colloquial situations. This might not be easy as it is not always possible to meet native English speakers to practise English with.

Studying in the UK can be hard work, but it is also very rewarding. Although the experience can be difficult, students often look back on their university days with happiness.

Exercise 3

The first part of the piece of reflective writing sets the scene by describing what happened. The final paragraph demonstrates that the student is able to *reflect* on what happened. The underlined parts of paragraph 3 show the language the student uses to introduce what he/she has learned from his/her experience. This is what you should try to show in your own writing.

<u>Looking back</u> at those notes, <u>I can see why</u> I reacted the way I did, but now that I have more background information about my group member, <u>I also understand</u> why she behaved the way she did. <u>I need to think about</u> why I acted so aggressively towards her missing the deadline and also why I took the argument so personally. There will inevitably be disagreements in professional life, and <u>I need to find a way of</u> managing them well. <u>I also need to think about</u> how I can show I am not very happy about something without upsetting the other person too much.

Chapter 10

Quiz Self-evaluation

1 If you would rather study with other people than on your own, then you should join a study group. This chapter will help you to think about how you can do this in the most effective way.

2 It is very likely that there are other people on your course who would like to study in a group but have not yet met the right people. This chapter will give you some ideas on how to meet them.

3 It might be a good idea to form a study group with people who are not your friends so you will spend the time studying and not socialising.

4 If you prefer to study on your own, then that is what you should do. But it is a good idea to work through the chapter to understand what the benefits of studying with others can bring as you might change your mind.

5 Other students can be a valuable source of support for you. You will have to give your presentation in front of a lot of people, so you should make use of any support you can.

6 Individual work is for individual students, but that does not mean you cannot share ideas with each other.

Exercise 1

1 **Advantages:** You can choose who to ask, so you do not have to ask people you have doubts about.

   Disadvantages: It might take a long time to ask a lot of people. People are often in a hurry before and after lectures.

2 **Advantages:** You can get your message to a lot of people very quickly and easily.

   Disadvantages: Everybody will get the message. You might be approached by too many students, or you might be approached by students you do not want to study with.

3 **Advantages:** It is easy to arrange, and a lot of people might see it. Also, you do not have to speak to a lot of people.

   Disadvantages: People might not see it and you might not get any responses. On the other hand, you might get too many responses.

4 **Advantages:** You do not have to try and stop people and talk to them. It is easy and convenient. You can choose who to give the invitation to.

   Disadvantages: Students might not respond for all sorts of reasons, including losing the invitation.

5 **Advantages:** It is a quick and easy way to get the message to a lot of students.

   Disadvantages: Everybody sees the email, so you cannot choose who will respond to it. You might get too many responses.

Exercise 2

1 **Don't:** This just encourages students to be lazy and use the group rather than contributing to it.

2 **Do:** By having some rules, students are more likely to be ready to work when they arrive.

3 **Don't:** Running things in an organized way helps the group to become more organized.

4 **Do:** This is similar to point 3. It also makes things less confusing.

5 **Don't:** Although it is a good idea to spend the first five minutes socialising, this should be kept to a minimum so that you do not lose sight of the purpose of the meeting.

6 **Do:** By insisting on such arrangements, group members are more likely to be committed to the group.

7 **Don't:** This not only takes time, but encourages students to use rather than contribute to the group.

8 **Do:** Unless there is a leader, there will be nobody to insist on the rules being implemented.

9 **Do:** This will give each group member a chance to prepare for the next meeting.

10 **Do:** This will make it even more likely that group members will prepare for the next meeting.

Exercise 3

1 **B:** This makes it more likely that you will follow the lecture. You will think of more questions as a group. And if you still have unanswered questions, you can bring them up at the next group meeting.

2 **D:** Obviously, you should take your own notes during a lecture, but it is also a good time to clarify things you are not sure about with a group member.

3 **D:** Again, this can only be done during the lecture. But instead of everyone recording the lecture, you could delegate this to a different group member and have them listen to it before the next meeting. Bear in mind that listening to a lecture takes as long as the lecture itself and can be very time-consuming for one person to do all the time.

4 **A:** It is more likely that you will make use of a recorded lecture if you deal with it as a group.

5 **B:** It is always easier to remember vocabulary when you put some effort into the process. Once again, doing this as a group adds an extra dimension to the process.

6 **A:** This is very useful if you find it difficult to 'see the wood for the trees'. It is easy to miss the point of a lecture, and this will affect your understanding of the topic unless you deal with it.

7 **B:** You get more from a lecture if you put something into it, and it is easier to do this as part of a group.

8 **B:** This relates to point 7 and might influence your choice of reading.

Exercise 4

1 **Good practice:** Everybody benefits from reading and discussing the ideas.

2 **Poor practice:** Students should all read *the whole of* the core text.

3 **Good practice:** Everybody benefits from reading and seeing what other students think is important.

4 **Good practice:** But it is important to do as much *extra* reading as you can on your own.

5 **Bad practice:** It is very unlikely that the notes other students have made on something *you* have not read will be helpful to you.

Exercise 5

Here are some more example questions.

- Is my pronunciation clear?

- Do I have good eye contact?

- Do I engage the audience?

- Is there a clear structure to my presentation?

- Do I use signposting language?

- Do I make any grammar mistakes?

- Have I got enough references?

- Do I have an adequate conclusion?

- How are my visual aids?

Exercise 6

All the activities could be used to improve your discussion skills. Use those you like, and try to adapt the others to suit you and your group.

Chapter 11

Quiz self-evaluation

1 It is true that online work can often be done when and where you want. But it is still *work*, and you should have a professional attitude towards it.

2 You will not be working online all the time. Depending on the task, you might spend a lot of time working on your own offline, for example reading, researching, thinking and writing. But you will need to spend *some* time online, communicating with other group members and sharing your work.

3 You will need to make an effort to get to know your online group members. This chapter will help you to do that.

4 It is even more important to meet deadlines when you work with a group online. You should therefore give yourself time to check and review your work before the deadline. Leaving work to the last minute is asking for trouble.

5 It *is* easy to get distracted when you are working on computers. You need to be disciplined and this is an important skill to learn.

Exercise 1

1 You *can* get to know people you do not meet face to face. If you have not worked closely with others online, you might be surprised how quickly you can bond with them. Use the 'getting to know you' activities in this chapter and in earlier chapters to speed up this process.

2 It is true that when team members do not come online, you have no idea what is happening. That is why it is so important to have rules about meeting and staying in touch.

3 Students who are doing an online module with a reputable university should have proper internet access. However, if your access *is* restricted, then you need to be very organized and make sure you do your offline work when there is no access in order to make full use of your online time.

4 All the students in your group should have adequate computer skills. You might have to

help each other to *improve* your skills, but this can be done *together*, which is one of the benefits of group work.

5 It probably *does* take a bit longer to collaborate online than face to face, but you save time in other ways.

6 It is true that misunderstandings are more likely online, which is why you need to be careful about saying things or making jokes that can be taken the wrong way.

7 It can sometimes take people a long time to respond to something online, so you have to wait before you move on. As in point 2, that is why it is important to have rules about staying in touch. A good rule is to respond to emails immediately, even if only to acknowledge receipt of the email and say when you will respond fully.

8 It can be difficult to find convenient times to meet when people are in different time zones. You might want to take it in turns to get up early or stay up late to make this work.

9 This is probably not true. Your online group should be as supportive as other groups.

10 This is exactly the same in all kinds of group work. Look back at previous chapters to help you to think about how you can manage students who are not contributing as much as they should.

11 This is not true, but students should make sure they share their workloads and help each other if one student seems to have too much to do.

12 This shows the importance of setting deadlines well in advance of submission time and making sure you stick to them.

Exercise 2

1 Yes, this is true most of the time and can be a major benefit.

2 Yes, being online is a good chance for less confident people to build their confidence.

3 Yes, but you should make sure you use this extra response time to make your contributions really worthwhile.

4 Yes, so you should see this as an *opportunity* to improve as many of your skills as you can. Most people need a *reason* for doing things, and online working provides a very good reason.

5 Yes, hard work will have an impact on a wide range of teamwork skills, so it is an excellent opportunity to improve them. And having to work harder does not mean that the work is less enjoyable; in fact it can be *more* enjoyable as you are more likely to feel a sense of achievement.

6 Yes, and by focusing on the content you are more likely to collaborate effectively and produce better results.

Exercise 3

All these activities are excellent ways of getting to know your online group members. Discuss the different activities with your group and choose some of them to do. Make sure you are all happy to do the activities or they will not work well.

Chapter 12

Quiz self-evaluation

1 There are many reasons for going back over work that you have done. It will help you to notice how you could have done the work better and what you could do next time to take into account what you have learned.

2 Unfortunately, your lecturer does not have time to give you an individualised learning plan. All students have different learning needs and should spend time finding out what those needs are.

3 Your course certainly cannot cover everything you need to know. There will always be some things that it is not possible to cover in the course. However, you will probably be able to access resources in the university that will help you to learn the skills and subject knowledge that are not covered.

4 Although this is probably true, it is still a good idea to be aware of your weaknesses so that you can try to address them. Although you cannot be perfect, you can always improve.

5 This is understandable, and it is not a good idea to overwork. However you should be a lifelong learner, someone who is always ready to learn new things.

Exercise 1

Completing a group work evaluation form should help you to reflect on what you did, why you did it, and what you learned. Most importantly, it should help you to realize what things you still need to work on and how you will do things differently next time.

Everybody's group work evaluation form will be different.

Exercise 2

Working through a skills audit review encourages you to think about specific skills that you had hoped to improve during your group work. Now is the time to consider what improvements you made and what improvements you want to continue to make.

Everybody's skills audit review will be different.

Exercise 3

1 Qavitha took on the responsibility of booking the room for group meetings, getting the key and emailing the information to the group.

2 She struggled with open-ended questions in her research methodology.

3 She went to her personal tutor and asked for help.

4 Qavitha talks about her language difficulties. She found it hard to answer questions directly and found the accent hard.

5 Friends helped her. Probably they were students, but it is not clear if they were home or international students.

6 The point Qavitha is making is that you get many different perspectives on things when you work in a group, as well as different ideas.

7 Qavitha gives the example of revising for exams with a group.

8 Patience.

9 In the long run it was probably beneficial because it meant that the group had to find a solution and move on. Without the argument there might have been no progress.

10 Even though the experience was not very pleasant, it was still a useful experience that Qavitha can reflect on and learn from.

Further comments and analysis

You may like to match the comment and analysis to the part of the interview it relates to.

1 Notice how Qavitha supported her group by volunteering for a responsibility. She was pro-active and showed good teamworking skills.

2 Qavitha found the work difficult but she did not struggle on her own. She went to her personal tutor for help, and he was happy to support her.

3 Home students can be a great source of support for international students. As an international student you should do what you can to meet home students as much as possible. They will also benefit from your experience, skills and the different outlook that you bring to things.

4 Lecturers will organize group work for you, but they will not organize things like group revision sessions. Think about organizing a study group so you can gain the benefits of group work outside formal group assignments.

5 Qavitha really shows how group work can provide support because the group members are always there to help you and you will always have more ideas if you work in a group.

6 Qavitha shows a good understanding of the need to treat group members with respect. You need to listen carefully to everybody's ideas and try to include them in your group work if you can, even if you need to change them a bit.

7 Qavitha's group argued because they got frustrated at their lack of progress. They all had different ideas about what to do and they could not move forward. They solved their problem by discussion and agreeing to include everyone's ideas.

8 Qavitha was unlucky to be in a group with someone who demanded complete control over the group work. This can be a difficult situation to deal with. Her group allowed the dominant student to take control. Strong students can dominate individual students, but it is harder for them to dominate a whole group if the group works together.

Exercise 4

1 Chen approached another student and asked her to join with her in forming a group.

2 This probably had a very positive effect on the group and was a good start to the group work process.

3 Chen and her group compromised over the slides in their presentation.

4 They tried talking to the student who was always late to get her to improve her behaviour.

5 They could have reminded her about the rules for their group. The important thing is to keep trying to get unmotivated students to understand their responsibilities towards the group.

6 Chen thinks that you learn how different people think and are inspired to think in new ways yourself.

7 She thinks international students need courage to work with students from other countries.

8 She says that when you work with students from other countries, you can get a lot of different ideas and learn how other people think.

Further comments and analysis

You may like to match the comment and analysis to the part of the interview it relates to.

1 It can be very difficult for some international students to approach home students and students from other countries about forming a group. It is a good idea to try to make contact with such students early on in your course. Then you can build on the relationships as your course progresses.

2 Chen discusses the value of having a diverse group. Because Chen had students from different parts of the world in her group, it was easy to get a wide variety of input into the group work. The diversity of the group made the group work much easier than if they had all had the same background.

3 Chen and her group members volunteered to take on responsibility for parts of the group task. This demonstrated a good commitment to teamwork and helped strengthen the group.

4 Chen's description of the digital presentation issue is a very good example of different students wanting different things. Chen and her Chinese friend wanted a lot of words on the slides, whereas her other group members wanted short simple sentences on the slides. In the end the students compromised and they both changed their work a little to find a middle way.

5 Although Chen and her friends tried to talk to the group member who was always late, she did not change her behaviour. Even if this happens to you, you should continue to try to work with the difficult group member right up until the end of the task. Then you can gain the benefit of the difficult experience you have had.

6 Chen believes that through doing group work with students from different countries she got completely new ideas that she would never have thought of on her own.

7 This comment again shows that Chen learned that there are many different ways of doing things successfully.

8 Chen's final remarks summarize the value of working with others: you learn how different people think, and this means you learn a lot. In English-speaking universities this learning is considered to be very important.

Exercise 5

1 Helen gets her students to do a mini-presentation about group work before they start their proper group work task.

2 She thinks that when students sign their ground rules, they are consciously agreeing to behave in a certain way.

3 She thinks the key to a successful presentation is time management because the students have to meet up to prepare their presentation.

4 They learn to cooperate, to improve their teamwork skill, and how to allocate responsibilities. They also they become aware of their strengths and weaknesses.

5 She thinks that when students work in international groups, they learn to look at things from different viewpoints: that is what critical thinking entails.

6 Many students think it is fair to get an individual mark as well as a group mark.

7 It shows that groups can achieve more when they work together than individuals on their own.

8 No, but she thinks they should try to solve any problems on their own first.

Further comments and analysis

You may like to match the comment and analysis to the part of the interview it relates to.

1 Helen wants her students to think about the process of group work before they actually start on their group task. You may have a teacher who helps you to do this, or you may have to do it yourself. If you are well prepared for your group work, you are likely to make a better job of it and get a higher mark.

2 You may have a teacher who asks you to write ground rules for your group. You may even be given ground rules. Alternatively, your teacher might not address this issue. In this case it will be up to you and the other students in your group to agree to use ground rules. It is highly likely that group members will function more effectively with ground rules to guide their behaviour and to make them aware of their responsibilities towards the group.

3 Notice what Helen thinks makes a poor group presentation: when students work separately on the individual parts of the presentation and then put them together quickly before delivering it. It is important to make a group presentation which goes together well, not a series of individual presentations.

4 Helen believes that learning in mixed nationality groups can greatly enhance student learning. It may feel more difficult to work in a mixed nationality group at first, but the benefits to your learning in the long run can be considerable.

5 Helen thinks that group work improves students' critical-thinking skills.

Exercise 6

1 Pat does this because he thinks they will do it better. He assumes they will help each other.

2 He mentions personality clashes and unmotivated students.

3 Not at all.

4 He talks about being a good colleague as well as having good colleagues.

5 Because when things go wrong, you can learn a lot.

6 He thinks you should face up to the problem early rather than avoid it.

Further comments and analysis

You may like to match the comment and analysis to the part of the interview it relates to.

1 Both Pat and Helen put students in groups and give them their assignments well in advance. You should use the time you are given to start thinking about your assignment early on.

2 Pat thinks that in certain situations groups can outperform individuals. He expects his students to support each other and learn from each other.

3 Your lecturers understand that group work can be very challenging at times. That is one reason why they give it to you. They think that having to deal with unmotivated group members is a good opportunity for students to learn teamwork skills.

4 Pat and Helen's different approaches to ground rules show there are differences in the ways lecturers do things. You need to read your assignment brief carefully to make sure you are following the guidelines. For example, if you are asked to draw up group ground rules but fail to do so, you are likely to lose marks.

5 The product of your group work does not always have to be a great success. The value of learning from group work lies in the experience. If you produce something that is not very good but you can show that you have learned a lot, you can still get a good mark. The teachers are interested in the process you went through and what skills you developed more than the product you ended up with.

6 Helen and Pat's comments show that they, like other teachers in English-speaking universities, believe that group work is an important learning tool for their students. They want their students to understand the value of group work, engage in group work, and then reflect on their experience to show what they have learned.

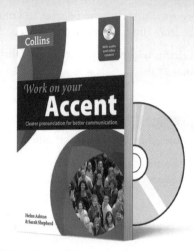